This book is a gift from:

Michael & Erin Aubrey

It is the hope and prayer of our family that this book will help you to lead more people to the Lord Jesus Christ and to help them grow strong in their Christian life.

To Seek and To Save

winning and building committed
followers of Jesus Christ

To Seek and To Save

winning and building committed
followers of Jesus Christ

Dr. Paul Chappell

Sword of the Lord Publishers

P. O. Box 1099, Murfreesboro, TN 37133

Dedication

This book is dedicated to the members of Lancaster Baptist Church. In response to God's grace at work in their hearts, they compassionately and consistently obey the Great Commission in their daily lives.

In particular, this text is dedicated to Jerry Ferrso, a friend and colaborer, who has owned the vision and is faithfully leading our soul-winning ministry into the twenty-first century.

Contents

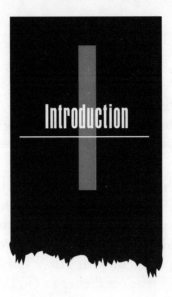

Introduction

Preparing

for a new millennium

As we approach a new millennium, there has been a renewed emphasis in Christendom on church growth. The phenomenon of the so-called "mega-churches" has intrigued many, and in many respects these are exciting days for local churches around the world.

The book you hold in your hands is not a book about church growth. It is possible today to grow a church without fulfilling the Great Commission! Jesus Christ did not call us to go into all the world and build churches. We are called to lead others to the Saviour and disciple them with His Word; church growth is merely the result of true obedience to God's command.

As we look at the matter of soul winning and evangelism, we must look from God's vantage point. Christ came to the earth "to seek and to save" the lost, and the fact remains—He is still seeking the lost. When God described His perspective on the Gentile world, He stated, *"They are all gone out of the way, they are together become unprofitable; there is none that doeth good, no, not one"* (Rom. 3:12). Certainly some men are seeking the truth about Christ on their own; and while those who are seeking are promised that they will find, those who are not seeking have to be sought.

Mankind as a whole has never sought after God, yet in His unending mercy, God has lovingly been seeking a restored fellowship with mankind since the Garden of Eden. The Bible clearly states, *"We love him, because he first loved us"* (I John 4:19). God is and has always been the Prime Mover in the matter of salvation; and when God took human form and came to the earth, He simplified His mission by stating, *"The Son of man is come to seek and to save that which was lost"* (Luke 19:10). God was now moving out and providing redemption through Christ. Jesus is truly the Seeker of men as well as the Saviour of men.

After redemption's work was accomplished, the Saviour left clear instructions for those who would establish His church. His commands did not revolve around a philosophy of preparing services specifically for people who were seeking the truth. He knew the heart of man, and He instructed us to continue His mission by becoming seekers of the lost ourselves. We are commanded to seek the lost in our own Jerusalem, Judea, Samaria, and the uttermost part of the earth. Jesus said, *"As my Father hath sent me, even so send I you."*

Of course, we are not saviours. We are just sinners who have been "bought with a price," but as we go and witness of the Saviour, the Holy Spirit (the true soul winner) draws men to Christ through the power of God's Word.

No doubt church services should be relevant and should uplift God's redemption through Christ; however, many Christians' ministries never extend beyond what they do inside the doors of their churches. I do not say this to belittle the efforts of anyone in his Christian ministry, but we must not shirk the convicting call of God on each of our lives to *"go out into the highways and hedges, and compel them...."*

Someone once said, "Tell me, and I'll forget; show me, and I'll remember; involve me, and I'll understand." The goal of this book is to train people to be soul winners by challenging them to get involved in the task of leading others to Christ. His return is imminent! We must not squander these last days of harvest for the Saviour. May God bless you as you set out to serve Him.

chapter
ONE

Principles

of soul winning

"The fruit of the righteous is a tree of life;
and he that winneth souls is wise."—
Prov. 11:30.

Soul winning is a subject closer to our Lord's heart than any other, yet it is perhaps the most neglected subject in the church today.

In the place of true soul winning, we are now finding so-called "lifestyle evangelism," or "bridge-building," or Athletes for Christ, or maybe even a Jog-a-thon for Jesus. One-on-one witnessing is taking a backseat to mass evangelism, citywide campaigns, televangelism and radio evangelism. Though these may not be wrong in themselves, many times Christians use them as a sort of "novocaine" to help them feel as if they have obeyed God, when truthfully they have neglected the Biblical command to tell others about Jesus face-to-face. Soul winning is personally sharing the Good News with another in the power of the Holy Spirit and then seeing that individual bow his head to confess his need for a Saviour and receive Jesus Christ into his heart.

The Mandate of Soul Winning

"Go ye therefore, and teach all nations, baptizing them in the name of the Father, and of the Son, and of the Holy Ghost: Teaching them to observe all things whatsoever I have commanded you: and, lo, I am with you alway, even unto the end of the world. Amen."—Matt. 28:19, 20.

An Authoritative Mandate

Soul winning is not a spiritual gift, nor is it an option; it is a mandate from God to every believer. A few might say, "That sounds like legalism! That sounds like something I am forced to do." They can call it what they will, but that does not change the fact that God Almighty demands that His people be soul winners. Before His ascension, Christ met with these believers and gave them an *authoritative mandate: "All power is given unto me in heaven and in earth. Go ye therefore...."*

On occasion one of my children might say to another, "Pick up your clothes," or "Straighten up your room." And I have heard the brother or sister reply something like, "Says who?" Likewise, when a preacher preaches, a Christian may ask, "Says who?" When it comes to soul winning, the answer to that question is very clear. Christ, who holds all things in His hands and who possesses all power, says, *"Go ye therefore...."*

Christians must operate on the foundation of the Lord's sovereign authority, the authority found in the words, *"All power is given unto me....Go ye therefore...."* Christ and His Word form the basis of our faith and direction. When it comes to preaching the Gospel, we are mandated by a sovereign God to go into all the world and preach it. It is an authoritative mandate.

An Active Mandate

Mark 16:15, just as inspired as any other portion of Scripture, reads, *"And he said unto them, Go ye into all the world, and preach the gospel to every creature."* And to the apostles He commanded in Acts 5:20, *"Go, stand and speak in the temple to the people all the words of this life."* A Christian cannot fulfill the mandate of soul winning by simply being involved in some form of a ministry; he can only fulfill it if he will "go" and talk to someone about Christ.

An Absolute Mandate

Absolute means "perfect in quality and nature, or complete." God's mandate for soul winning has three distinct parts which we must obey, follow, and fulfill completely if we truly intend to do what God has commanded us to do: 1) to go win souls to Christ, 2) to baptize them, 3) to teach them God's Word.

Disciples fulfill the first of these commands to "go...and teach all nations" through preaching the Word of God.

"Now they which were scattered abroad upon the persecution that arose about Stephen travelled as far as Phenice, and Cyprus, and Antioch, preaching the word to none but unto the Jews only. And some...when they were come to Antioch, spake unto the Grecians, preaching the Lord Jesus. And the hand of the Lord was with them: and a great number believed, and turned unto the Lord."—Acts 11:19–21.

The hand of the Lord was with the early church as they preached Christ to their world. As a result of their preaching, many believed and turned to the Lord. When a man turns to the Lord, he turns from his idols to serve the living and true God. If we will speak the Word and teach all nations, we will see men and women genuinely turn to Christ in faith, not just for an insurance policy from Hell.

The first step of obedience after the salvation experience is water baptism, which is a public testimony of a man's personal faith in Christ. Perhaps someone may ask, "Who says I have to be baptized?" Acts 2:41 states, *"Then they that gladly received his word were baptized."* Jesus desires His children to identify publicly with His death, burial and resurrection. It is one thing to put a little fish on a bumper sticker or to wear a cross around the neck, but it is another thing to identify publicly with Christ in believer's baptism.

> It is possible to lead men to Christ, baptize them, disciple them, and involve them in soul winning!

After we lead people to Christ and baptize them, we must disciple them. Matthew 28:20 says, *"Teaching them to observe all things whatsoever I have commanded you."* Many churches lead others to Christ but never stress obedience in baptism. Other churches might baptize many yet never strive to help them grow in the Word of God through a Bible class or some form of discipling. Other churches might occupy all their time discipling small groups of Christians while neglecting opportunities to tell the lost masses about Christ. Is it possible to lead men to Christ, baptize them, disciple them, and involve them in soul winning? By the grace of God—yes, it is!

An Accompanied Mandate

When we finally give in and say, "All right, Lord, I'm going out on visitation," or "Lord, I'll go to talk to my neighbor tomorrow," or "Lord, I will call my loved ones tonight and tell them about Christ," we are not alone. Christ promised, *"Lo, I am with you alway."*

Many times I have gone witnessing in areas infested with crime and open sin. I have also encountered some tough situations when I was physically alone; however, I really was not alone because the Lord was there with me. In those times when fear might have crept in and hindered the Lord's work, what a blessing it was to remember this promise!

When G. Campbell Morgan came upon the words, *"Lo, I am with you alway,"* while reading Scripture to female shut-ins in a convalescent home, he commented to them, "Isn't that a wonderful promise!" One dear woman replied, "No, it's a reality!" Christ's presence is a reality, not just words in a promise. That reality ought to make us approach soul winning with more boldness than ever before.

The Motive of Soul Winning

Does motive really matter in soul winning? Jeremiah 17:10 reads, *"I the LORD search the heart."* God sees what every nursery worker, Sunday school worker, choir member, preacher and bus worker does each weekend, and He sees the heart attitude as it is done. We read in Psalm 139:1, *"O LORD, thou hast searched me, and known me."* Christians not only need to make the decision to be soul winners, but they also need to make the decision to have the right motives for soul winning.

Even the Apostle Paul had to make sure that he had proper motives for his works. Because motives were important, he spent much time sharing and defending his motives for his ministry.

In I Thessalonians 2:3–6 Paul clarifies his motives:

"For our exhortation was not of deceit, nor of uncleanness, nor in guile: But as we were allowed of God to be put in trust with the gospel, even so we speak; not as pleasing men, but God, which trieth our hearts. For neither at any time used we flattering words, as ye know, nor a cloke of covetousness; God is witness: Nor of men sought we glory, neither of you, nor yet of others, when we might have been burdensome, as the apostles of Christ."

Paul's purpose at Thessalonica was not to build the world's largest church or to achieve fame and recognition; he went there to glorify the Lord. One reason that God blessed his work was that he had pure motives. If we are motivated by personal gain, recognition or pleasing those around us, our efforts will not have God's blessing.

Our purpose in soul winning should not be to get what we can out of it or to build a big church. The Lord will build the church as a result of Christians' being motivated solely by their love for Him and their desire to glorify Him. Actually, we are not even the real soul winners: the Holy Spirit is. We are just the "delivery boys" of the Good News. If our motive for delivering the message of Christ is anything other than pleasing its Author and carrying out His will, we fail.

Christ—Our Example

There is not a purer example in Scripture to pattern our motives after than the example of Christ Himself. *"For the Son of man is come to seek and to save that which was lost"* (Luke 19:10). Since the Saviour personally went looking for the lost, brought them to a saving knowledge of Himself, and told them of a home in Heaven, then each Christian should follow in His steps with a pure heart to lead the lost to Christ.

You may ask, "What are some examples of pure motives?" One thing that motivated Christ was the brevity of time. In John 4:35 He tells us, *"Say not ye, There are yet four months, and then cometh harvest? behold, I say unto you, Lift up your eyes, and look on the fields; for they are white already to harvest."* The Lord acknowledged the urgency of bringing in the harvest while there was yet time. How much more should we who are living two thousand years later be motivated to follow His pattern of soul winning!

Not only was Christ motivated by urgency but also by an intense desire to please His Father in Heaven.

One time a pastor who drove me to the airport said to me, "You know, Brother Chappell, you are an intense man." I'm not sure whether that was a compliment or not! You can call me "intense," but as long as souls are lost, as long as the fields are white unto harvest, as long as people can be reached who are within the sound of my voice and the influence of my life, I will tell them about salvation through Jesus Christ. It is time Christians got a dose of holy intensity about sharing the Gospel.

There is no higher purpose than looking on the fields of harvest with the same urgency and intensity that the Saviour did as He walked this earth. Someday soon, when the trump of God sounds, I will never regret having shared the Gospel.

What made the situation so urgent to Christ? He knew that there was a literal Hell, and He referred to it in His preaching more than He did any other single subject. In Luke 16:23 He spoke about a man who was in the lake of fire: *"And in hell he lift up his eyes, being in torments."* Someone may ask me, "Why all the intensity?" or "Why are you in such a hurry?" Because there is a literal Hell of torments and fire where men and women are crying out. Everyone who does not accept Christ will spend eternity in that terrible place. If that will not motivate you to win souls, nothing will.

Three months before God led me to pastor in southern California, I heard a message about Hell, and God convicted me that day that if there was no other reason to be a soul winner, no other motive, the reality of Hell was reason and motive enough.

Once we develop the urgency and the intensity that we need for soul winning, it is amazing how the Holy Spirit leads and positions us as Christians in the very spot where someone is ripe unto harvest.

Several years ago, I was out running some errands. At the time I was driving an old, run-down, white Toyota. Suddenly the car began jerking and lunging, as it had done in the past; but it so happened that this time it broke down right in front of the Dodge

> Someday soon, when the trump of God sounds, I will never regret having shared the Gospel.

dealership. I was somewhat humored by the thought that this could be a sign from God to buy a new car!

So, I walked into that car dealership and began to look for a good price on a car. Then, there it was, that Dodge minivan. It looked right; it smelled right; it handled so well during the test drive. It had all the gizmos that make no difference yet seem to add another ten percent to the price of the car. I was never going to tilt the seat that way anyway, but just knowing I could, made it worth more.

After all the emotional buildup, the salesman and I went inside the little "sell block." All of the friendly questions followed: "You want something to drink?" "Can I help you with anything?" "Is it cool enough?" He wanted this sale with a passion.

As he started to bring me in for the kill, God laid something on my heart. Obviously not in an audible voice, the Holy Spirit seemed to say, "If you care as much about his soul as he cares about selling you this car, he might get saved." Right then all the excitement about the car faded, and I became very calm.

I said, "Hey, Ralph, wait one second."

"Yes, what is it?"

"Ralph, this car is great. I've never seen seats do what these can do. It's really something. But first let me ask you a question. Ralph, if you were to die today, would you go to Heaven, to Hell, or do you know?"

He looked at me as if I had just landed from Mars. I told him I was a Baptist pastor. He listened to every word as I went through the Romans Road salvation verses with him. We were in the "sell block"; my old car was going nowhere, and neither was Ralph.

I wish I could tell you that Ralph got saved that day, but I can't. After awhile, the manager came in and said, "Hey, Ralph, what are we having here, church or what?" We had to return to the contract and to the car purchase.

After I purchased the car, I handed the church brochure to Ralph and said, "Ralph, here in this brochure are the verses which I just shared with you that will show you how to accept Jesus Christ as Saviour. Here is my home number; be sure to call if you need help."

I drove my new Dodge van home. At about one o'clock that next morning, the phone rang. I'm not very good at phone calls at one o'clock in the morning! Finally I woke up, and the voice on the other end said, "Hello, this is Ralph. We talked today."

About then I realized who Ralph was. He continued, "You know, today you asked me a question: If I died, would I go to Heaven or to Hell, or did I know? I just can't get to sleep. Could we get together and talk?"

I didn't say, "Well, listen, I work eight to five in the ministry." Rather, I said, "I think Denny's is open; I'll meet you there in thirty minutes."

When Ralph and I met, we went through the Scriptures again. I will never forget his salvation. I told him, "Ralph, right now, in the privacy of this booth, all you need to do is simply bow your head, pray and tell the Lord that you know you are a sinner, that you need a Saviour; and then if you will call upon Him, He will come into your life and save you."

Ralph responded, "All right, let's pray." He folded his hands, and with people all around and waitresses going back and forth, he prayed, "Dear Lord, I just want to thank You for this man talking to me today," and he went on to talk to the Lord and to receive Him as Saviour. Needless to say, I rejoiced as he prayed.

Sometime when you pray, go up to a mountain or find a high spot somewhere, and look out over all the homes and buildings, and ask God to help you get burdened for the people like Ralph who live where you live yet are on their way to a literal, burning Hell. And then when God lays a person on your heart that He wants you to witness to, obey the Holy Spirit.

The Ministry of a Soul Winner

To Be Effective—Be a Faithful Christian

What do Christians have to do to become effective soul winners? Jesus went to the disciples and simply said, *"Follow me, and I will make you fishers of men."* One reason Christians are ineffective and sporadic in soul winning is that they have failed to realize that an effective soul winner must, first and foremost, be a faithful Christian. He must be a disciple, a follower of Christ, one who 'abides in the shadow of the Almighty,' and one who walks in the presence of God. One who communes with God does not soon lose the fervor, the vision, the desire, nor the compassion for the lost.

Jesus said, *"Follow me, and I will make you fishers of men"* (Matt. 4:19). Soul winning alone does not equal spirituality, but a spiritual Christian will always be a soul winner.

To Be Effective—Be a Filled Christian

Second, a soul winner is filled with the Holy Spirit.

"But ye shall receive power, after that the Holy Ghost is come upon you: and ye shall be witnesses unto me both in Jerusalem, and in all Judæa, and in Samaria, and unto the uttermost part of the earth."—Acts 1:8.

One reason that the Holy Spirit has been given to Christians is for power to witness for Christ. He will teach and guide us even in the act of witnessing. Then He brings about the process of regeneration, where someone is spiritually **re-gened** or "born again," as we say, and is brought into the family of God. John 16:13, 14 says, *"Howbeit when he, the Spirit of truth, is come, he will guide you into all truth...will shew you things to come. He shall glorify me."* The Holy Spirit will 'guide us into all truth' in order to accomplish the highest purpose of all, to glorify Christ.

My wife, Terrie, and I often enjoy going together and telling others about the Lord. One day we went to a house where we began talking to a family who had just moved up from North Hollywood.

Though they had a church background, I asked if they knew for sure that if they died they would go to Heaven. Do you know the answer I got? "Well, probably." I had to do a little more "research" on that one! The second time around, it was, "You know, maybe not."

The average Christian might have said, "Well, we'll just go now." But when you are concerned about someone's staying out of Hell, you are not going to settle for "Well, probably," or "Ah, maybe." You want the saved to say, "Yes, I am going to Heaven." About an hour later that couple bowed to pray and accepted Christ as their Saviour.

If you and I are not following Christ, if we are not filled with the Holy Spirit, if we are cantankerous with one another, if we are up and down, if we are just kind of in and out with our spiritual walk, nothing will happen when we try to witness. But if we follow Christ, are filled with His Spirit, and go in His power, then we will come back rejoicing, bringing our sheaves with us.

In the early part of the twentieth century, a group of preachers met to discuss a citywide campaign. One preacher said, "I think we should have D. L. Moody for the campaign." Another spoke up and said, "Why should it be D. L. Moody? Does he have a monopoly on the Holy Spirit?" The other said, "No, but the Holy Spirit has a monopoly on D. L. Moody." We need to allow the Holy Spirit to have a monopoly on us.

To Be Effective—Be a Faithful Witness

Third, I have found that a soul winner who is following Christ and filled with the Spirit will be a *faithful* witness.

In Acts 20:20 Paul taught publicly from house to house. Only one percent of all churches in America grew by ten percent in 1994. One reason I believe God is blessing Lancaster Baptist Church is that our members believe that God gave a mandate to His children and that we are to take this mandate with the right motives and follow the right pattern for ministry. We are to go out into a community and reach others for Jesus Christ.

In the last five years the people of the Lancaster Baptist Church averaged knocking on more than five hundred doors a day for an entire year. That is over two hundred thousand doors per year. You see what can happen when a group of people obey God? What method does God bless to build His church in the nineties? The same method He blessed in the first century—His people faithfully witnessing, *"publickly, and from house to house."*

Never underestimate the tract that you pass out or the word that you say. God's Word will never "return void," and the promise of Scripture is still true: *"They that sow in tears shall reap in joy."*

"They that sow in tears shall reap in joy. He that goeth forth and weepeth, bearing precious seed, shall doubtless come again with rejoicing, bringing his sheaves with him."—
Ps. 126:5, 6.

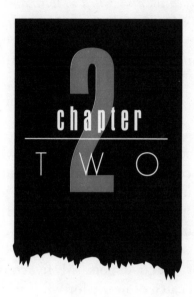

chapter
TWO

Preparation

for soul winning

"Who hath saved us, and called us with an holy calling, not according to our works, but according to his own purpose and grace, which was given us in Christ Jesus before the world began."—II Tim. 1:9.

I can remember one day as a young boy, while visiting family in Colorado, my cousins and I walked up the mountain to go trout fishing. My cousins had all of the proper gear and knew what the purpose of each piece was. They discussed their favorite spots along the creek, and each had a spot that he preferred. Unlike my cousins, I had a small fishing pole and very little knowledge of trout fishing or of "the good spots." My five cousins brought home a combined total catch of nearly forty fish that day, while I, "the city kid," caught one trout! Why? Because I had not met the prerequisites of a prepared fisherman.

Any Christian can witness with the Holy Spirit's power, but why then are some Christians more effective soul winners than others? Could it be that they are better prepared? As Christians, we need to remember that we are at war here on this earth against principalities, powers and the rulers of the darkness of this world (Eph. 6:12). Soul winners are not just ambassadors; they are soldiers fighting a spiritual battle on the front lines and in the trenches. Does a soldier go into battle unprepared? If he does, he might be helping the enemy and not even know it.

The Salvation Day

One major weapon that is necessary in this battle is a clear understanding of what really happened on our own salvation day.

In II Corinthians 3:18–4:1, the Apostle Paul testifies that our ministry starts on the day of our salvation. He states, *"But we all, with open face beholding as in a glass the glory of the Lord, are changed into the same image from glory to glory, even as by the Spirit of the Lord. Therefore seeing we have this ministry, as we have received mercy, we faint not."*

The Bible promises to all who are born again not only an eternity in Heaven but also an entirely new existence. Paul wrote in II Corinthians 5:17, *"Therefore if any man be in Christ, he is a new creature: old things are passed away; behold, all things are become new."* What a tragedy if a man were not to experience newness of life and a change of destiny after accepting Jesus Christ as Saviour!

If a man becomes a new creature in Christ, his goals should be redirected by the Holy Spirit. First Corinthians 3:16 states, *"Know ye not that ye are the temple of God, and that the Spirit of God dwelleth in you?"* At the point of salvation, a person is indwelt by the Holy Spirit of God, whose desire is to lead that Christian and to guide him into all truth. Christ Himself promised in John 16:13: *"Howbeit when he, the Spirit of truth, is come, he will guide you into all truth: for he shall not speak of himself; but whatsoever he shall hear, that shall he speak: and he will shew you things to come."*

Ephesians 2:19 explains that in addition to receiving the Holy Spirit, at salvation we literally become citizens of Heaven. *"Now therefore ye are no more strangers and foreigners, but fellowcitizens with the saints, and of the household of God."* Just as the citizens of America have rights, privileges and responsibilities, so do citizens of Heaven. As Americans have a physical and mental obligation to their country, a Christian has a spiritual obligation to his Lord. To the unsaved, these responsibilities might seem ludicrous; however, a Christian should see it as his "reasonable service" (Rom. 12:1). He should now desire to serve his Lord and Saviour inwardly with a pure heart and motive, and outwardly with obedience to the commands of God. It is a joy to me to know that I have a spiritual purpose and objective in this life, that I have been called according to His purpose.

There are three fundamental aspects of every salvation experience. The process begins with the **transmission of spiritual truth,** which results in a **change of mind** and a **truthful purpose** for the life of the individual.

The Transmission of Spiritual Truth

The day that a person accepts Jesus Christ as Saviour is the day that someone else cared enough about that person to share with him the most important truth that the world has ever known. The transmission of that life-changing message to all the lost of this world should be the primary objective of God's people today. Second Timothy 2:2 shows an example of how this task is a continual process in the ministry. *"And the things that **thou** hast heard of **me** among many witnesses, the same **commit** thou to **faithful men**, who shall be able to **teach others also.**"*

The word *thou* indicates the importance of the individual, and the word *me* indicates the personal nature of the contact. The verb *commit* suggests a transmitting of truth to a receiver. The receivers, here specified as *faithful men,* will then be responsible to *teach others also.* At this point the spiritual transmission begins to multiply! It is only when a Christian begins to develop those around him that his success in the ministry will become permanent.

A Change of Mind

Whenever a person is truly saved, a change of mind should be evident. This change will evidence itself in different ways and at different levels, depending on the individual, but true repentance should at some point and to some degree manifest itself in a desire to please the Lord.

One example of this desire is in Acts 22:1–11, where Paul is converted from a persecutor of the church to a preacher of the Gospel. Upon his salvation, his immediate question to the Lord was, *"And I said, What shall I do, Lord? And the Lord said unto me, Arise, and go into Damascus; and there it shall be told thee of all things which are appointed for thee to do."* Paul's salvation was evidenced by a desire to serve the Lord immediately.

A Truthful Purpose in Life

There are several passages which link salvation to the responsibility of the Christian life. While a person's salvation is not dependent upon works in any way, he does need to understand that with the gift of salvation comes responsibility.

"But we all, with open face beholding as in a glass the glory of the Lord, are changed into the same image from glory to glory, even as by the Spirit of the Lord. Therefore seeing we have this ministry, as we have received mercy, we faint not; But have renounced the hidden things of dishonesty, not walking in craftiness, nor handling the word of God deceitfully; but by manifestation of the truth commending ourselves to every man's conscience in the sight of God."—II Cor. 3:18–4:2.

"Who hath saved us, and called us with an holy calling, not according to our works, but according to his own purpose and grace, which was given us in Christ Jesus before the world began."—II Tim. 1:9.

"For even hereunto were ye called: because Christ also suffered for us, leaving us an example, that ye should follow his steps."—I Pet. 2:21.

In summary, a soul winner should understand his own salvation day as he prepares to share the Gospel with others.

Spiritual Prerequisites

The primary prerequisite for soul winning is that the soul winner be saved. Some people feel that they must complete several weeks of doctrine classes before they can tell someone how to become a Christian. That notion could not be further from the truth. Every Christian can win souls to Christ regardless of how long he has been saved, yet the fact is not disputed that some are much more effective than others. I believe, more often than not, the reason for this difference in effectiveness hinges on certain spiritual prerequisites that must be met to become an effective soul winner.

A Proper Life's Objective

One such prerequisite is that a Christian's objective in life should be **parallel to that which God has set forth in the Scriptures.** Matthew 6:33 says, *"But seek ye first the kingdom of God, and his righteousness; and all these things shall be added unto you."*

Willing to Pay a Price

Second Timothy 2:3, 4 explains that a soul winner should be **willing to pay any price** to have the will of God fulfilled in his life: *"Thou therefore endure hardness, as a good soldier of Jesus Christ. No man that warreth entangleth himself with the affairs of this life; that he may please him who hath chosen him to be a soldier."*

A Love for God's Word

The soul winner should have **a love for God's Word.** *"Thy words were found, and I did eat them; and thy word was unto me the joy and rejoicing of mine heart: for I am called by thy name, O LORD God of hosts"* (Jer. 15:16).

A Servant's Heart

He should also have **a servant's heart.** *"But it shall not be so among you: but whosoever will be great among you, let him be your minister; And whosoever will be chief among you, let him be your servant: Even as the Son of man came not to be ministered unto, but to minister, and to give his life a ransom for many"* (Matt. 20:26–28).

Putting No Confidence in the Flesh

A wise soul winner **puts no confidence in his flesh.** *"But we had the sentence of death in ourselves, that we should not trust in ourselves, but in God which raiseth the dead"* (II Cor. 1:9). He should have a genuine love for people. *"Herein is love, not that we loved God, but that he loved us, and sent his Son to be the propitiation for our sins. Beloved, if God so loved us, we ought also to love one another"* (I John 4:10, 11).

Avoiding Bitterness

This soul winner should **never be bitter.** *"Looking diligently lest any man fail of the grace of God; lest any root of bitterness springing up trouble you, and thereby many be defiled"* (Heb. 12:15).

Leading a Disciplined Life

He has learned to **live a disciplined life.** *"Know ye not that they which run in a race run all, but one receiveth the prize? So run, that ye may obtain. And every man that striveth for the mastery is temperate in all things. Now they do it to obtain a corruptible crown; but we an incorruptible. I therefore so run, not as uncertainly; so fight I, not as one that beateth the air: But I keep under my body, and bring it into subjection: lest that by any means, when I have preached to others, I myself should be a castaway"* (I Cor. 9:24–27).

These prerequisites are not rules; rather, they reflect the attitude of a Spirit-filled soul winner. Without them I cannot hope to become an effective soul winner. Every Christian should be striving daily to be successful in each of these areas.

The Cost of Soul Winning

Whenever an individual gains a privilege, in turn he gains a responsibility. When one receives the Lord as his personal Saviour, he receives many eternal blessings. With these blessings, he also receives a spiritual responsibility to serve God.

This responsibility is a type of Christian service which God intends to be a part of the new Christian's spiritual growth. God does not need a soul winner's help; a soul winner needs God's help. Soul winning is a responsibility given to a Christian for his own good. God certainly could have carried His message to the world through other means, but He chose to use His created people for the task.

Soul winning is an opportunity to learn to rely on the infinite resources of God. It is a chance to give one's life to something of great value rather than to something carnal or perishable.

Self-Sacrifice

The cost of this responsibility is the cost of self-sacrifice and the willingness to lose all in order to gain everything. We must be willing to sacrifice whatever would keep us from being dedicated to the task of soul winning. In the end, the benefits and the blessings of the Christian life will far exceed the cost.

> Soul winning is an opportunity to learn to rely on the infinite resources of God.

Jesus calls His disciples today just as He did nearly two thousand years ago. In Luke 9:23, 24, He said, *"If any man will come after me, let him deny himself, and take up his cross daily, and follow me. For whosoever will save his life shall lose it: but whosoever will lose his life for my sake, the same shall save it."* The successful soul winner will pay the cost of self-sacrifice and will be willing to deny himself. He will consistently serve God seven days a week.

"No man can serve two masters: for either he will hate the one, and love the other; or else he will hold to the one, and despise the other. Ye cannot serve God and mammon. Therefore I say unto you, Take no thought for your life, what ye shall eat, or what ye shall drink; nor yet for your body, what ye shall put on. Is not the life more than meat, and the body than raiment?"—Matt. 6:24, 25.

Christ plainly teaches that the cost of soul winning and Christian discipleship involves self-sacrifice. The Apostle Paul gives some specific principles and guidelines concerning self-sacrifice and Christian service. In II Timothy 2:1, 2 Paul says that the soul winner must be willing to share his faith, realizing that those without Christ are captives of Satan and that only the Gospel can free them from that captivity: *"Thou therefore, my son, be strong in the grace that is in Christ Jesus. And the things that thou hast heard of me among many witnesses, the same commit thou to faithful men, who shall be able to teach others also."*

Who can know how God will use us when we lay aside our own selfishness and petty preferences? A few years ago, I began witnessing to a salesman in a store. He was open to the Gospel but was unwilling to pray and receive Christ at that moment. I gave him my phone number and told him to call me at home anytime. A few weeks later, he called me at home on my day off, and I met him after his work shift at 9:00 p.m. Did I necessarily plan to spend my day off this way? Certainly not. But as I laid aside myself and went that night, God was able to use me to lead the gentleman to Christ. Later the man told me that the offer to call me anytime at home helped him know that I was sincere.

Self-sacrifice is a testimony to the lost that many times weighs much more than our words. The unsaved man will be moved by the testimony of a soul winner who pays the price of self-sacrifice.

Personal Separation

Because a soul winner is stepping forward as an example to the world, lack of personal separation from the world could be a major hindrance to his testimony and witness for Christ. *"Thou therefore endure hardness, as a good soldier of Jesus Christ. No man that warreth entangleth himself with the affairs of this life; that he may please him who hath chosen him to be a soldier"* (II Tim. 2:3, 4).

Potential Persecution

Although presently in the United States physical suffering for the Christian faith is very rare, the soul winner should always be prepared for the day when he may have to suffer physical persecution. *"Wherein I suffer trouble, as an evil doer, even unto bonds; but the word of God is not bound"* (II Tim. 2:9). When society becomes increasingly intolerant of Christianity, persecution always results. On the other hand, no soul winner should ever seek persecution or trouble in order to gain God's approval, but rather he should study and saturate himself with God's Word. *"Study to shew thyself approved unto God, a workman that needeth not to be ashamed, rightly dividing the word of truth"* (II Tim. 2:15).

> No soul winner should ever seek persecution or trouble in order to gain God's approval.

Personal Study

Because of the need to be ready to give an answer to all the pertinent questions, soul winners must become diligent students of the Word of God. Only the Word of God can give the soul winner the discernment that he needs. *"But shun profane and vain babblings: for they will increase unto more ungodliness"* (II Tim. 2:16). *"But foolish and unlearned questions avoid, knowing that they do gender strifes"* (II Tim. 2:23). In these verses the Word of God cautions us to avoid foolishness and divisiveness as we present the Gospel. Many times we are not successful in soul winning because we do not have the discernment to avoid foolish, religious debates and stay focused on preaching Christ. The Bible tells us to be *"determined not to know any thing…save Jesus Christ, and him crucified"* (I Cor. 2:2).

In addition to being students, we must be servants. Every soul winner should serve the Master gladly. *"And the servant of the Lord must not strive; but be gentle unto all men, apt to teach, patient"* (II Tim. 2:24). A sincere soul winner has a servant's heart and is willing to be a servant to all men in order to win some for Christ.

Each of these scriptural commands requires us to replace our own desires with God's desires. There must be a willingness on the part of each soul winner to understand this important fact before proceeding in his service to God through soul winning. The more sacrificially one gives of himself to the Lord, the more he will benefit spiritually as God uses him to accomplish His work.

Prayer and the Holy Spirit

A common misconception regarding soul winning is that someone can learn a little speech and in his own strength and charisma, be able to win people to the Lord. Some approach soul winning as a salesperson would approach a sale. A salesman can get a person to make a decision to buy a product, whether he truly believes in the product or not. A person cannot be saved without believing on the Lord Jesus Christ, and only the Holy Spirit can bring about that decision. Certainly we must learn principles about appearance and the presentation of facts, but we must never forget that it is the Holy Spirit of God who will ultimately do the convicting through the Word of God.

Jesus told His disciples that when He ascended into Heaven, the Holy Spirit would come to the earth and convict men of their sin: *"Nevertheless I tell you the truth; It is expedient for you that I go away: for if I go not away, the Comforter will not come unto you; but if I depart, I will send him unto you. And when he is come, he will reprove the world of sin, and of righteousness, and of judgment: Of sin, because they believe not on me; Of righteousness, because I go to my Father, and ye see me no more; Of judgment, because the prince of this world is judged"* (John 16:7–11).

Thus, the Spirit of God convicts the sinner, and the Word of God is the instrument which the Holy Spirit blesses. Romans 10:17 says, *"So then faith cometh by hearing, and hearing by the word of God."* The Bible calls the Word of God *"the sword of the Spirit"* (Eph. 6:17). God the Holy Spirit not only uses the written Word, but He uses men for the work of soul winning as well. The Bible commands every Christian, *"And be not drunk with wine, wherein is excess; but be filled with the Spirit"* (Eph. 5:18). The Holy Spirit does indwell every believer; however, not every believer is Spirit-filled. If a Christian is truly filled with the Holy Spirit, he will naturally be a soul winner.

A soul winner must continually be seeking the power and filling of the Holy Spirit.

A soul winner must continually be seeking the power and filling of the Holy Spirit in order to win others to Christ. He must be *"praying always with all prayer and supplication in the Spirit"* (Eph. 6:18). If the desire of his heart is to reach the souls of men and women, he must ask for the power of the Holy Spirit of God.

The Holy Spirit not only convicts the sinner and empowers the believer, but He also guides the soul winner in the truth of God's Word. *"Howbeit when he, the Spirit of truth, is come, he will guide you into all truth: for he shall not speak of himself; but whatsoever he shall hear, that shall he speak: and he will shew you things to come. He shall glorify me: for he shall receive of mine, and shall shew it unto you"* (John 16:13, 14).

Several years ago our church family was preparing for a new building program. Part of the program involved purchasing some property to subdivide into various parcels for future development purposes. To make sure we did everything by the book, we contacted an attorney in Thousand Oaks, California and set up a meeting to explain to him our situation.

As soon as I walked into that office, God immediately impressed upon my heart that my relationship with Richard Van Sickle, P. A., would be more than a professional relationship. From that very first meeting, I began to pray that God would use me to lead Richard to the Lord Jesus Christ.

After that first meeting, I wrote Richard a letter and included in it a brochure of the church which highlighted the Gospel plan of salvation. In subsequent meetings, I would always take time to explain portions of the Gospel and talk to Richard about what the Lord had done for him on Calvary. In the meantime, I added Richard's name to a prayer list of unsaved people that I keep to remind me to pray specifically for their salvation.

Finally, one spring our church was sponsoring a day called Open House Sunday. I invited Richard and his family to be my guests on that day, and to my delight, they accepted my invitation and attended our service. For many weeks prior to that day, I prayed that Richard would come to know Christ as his Saviour. As I preached the gospel message that morning, I noticed Richard was listening intently. During the time of public invitation, I prayed that he would come down to accept Christ. Although he did not respond to the invitation, I sensed God was working in a special way in Richard's heart.

After the service, I continued to pray for Richard and felt impressed of the Lord to ask him if he would give me a few moments of his time. His wife encouraged him to take a moment with me, so he agreed, and we made our way back into the auditorium which was now almost empty. Sensing that Richard's heart was ready to receive Christ, I got right to the point. "Richard, would you like to receive Christ now?" I asked. "Yes," he responded. After a brief review of God's plan of salvation, Richard received Christ.

Richard had helped the church in many ways in the past, but the joy from those small things paled in comparison to the greatest joy of all, seeing him accept Christ as Saviour. When I yielded myself to the prompting of God's Spirit, He took over. He not only empowered and led me as the soul winner, but He also convicted Richard and brought about the wonderful work of salvation in his life.

The Holy Spirit of God must be our only source of strength if we desire to see conversions in our personal soul-winning endeavors. The Spirit-filled missionary Hudson Taylor once said, "It is possible to love men, through God, by prayer alone." Every soul winner must seek God's burden for souls and God's power through the Holy Spirit to carry out His mandate of winning souls to Christ.

chapter

THREE

3

Principles

of the Gospel

"Therefore as by the offence of one judgment came upon all men to condemnation; even so by the righteousness of one the free gift came upon all men unto justification of life."—Rom. 5:18.

A thorough understanding of the gospel message is vital in soul winning. A soul winner cannot be effective with those who have never even heard the Gospel if he does not have a clear understanding of it himself. In addition, a *serious* soul winner had better be more than just "familiar" with the message of the Gospel. He must allow the Biblical truths literally to permeate his thoughts and change his desires. When the soul winner yields to the Spirit and becomes saturated with the Gospel, he can be a more effective soul winner for Christ.

Many Christians today are fearful of sharing the gospel message. Some claim it is too complicated and confusing and as a result shy away from any opportunity to share it. The truth of the matter is that the Gospel is a simple, clear and objective truth, and only our own inhibition and laziness stand in our way of learning it and becoming comfortable with sharing it. We cannot forget that this message is the answer for all men and women; therefore, we must be thoroughly competent at sharing this great truth. There are three primary truths of the Gospel that we must understand.

Man's Problem

At some point, a person must realize that there is nothing that he can do to obtain his own salvation. Only the true Gospel will completely transform his life. Salvation is not merely turning over a new leaf, practicing right thinking, denying self or performing good works. Salvation is the result of understanding this first basic

Biblical principle. No amount of good works will gain salvation for our souls. Only Christ's finished work on the cross brings salvation. These verses serve as a reminder of this truth.

"For by grace are ye saved through faith; and that not of yourselves: it is the gift of God: Not of works, lest any man should boast."—Eph. 2:8, 9.

"But we are all as an unclean thing, and all our righteousnesses are as filthy rags; and we all do fade as a leaf; and our iniquities, like the wind, have taken us away."—Isa. 64:6.

All Have Sinned

Before any individual can be saved, he must understand his need for a Saviour. The reason that all men need a Saviour is that the Bible teaches that all men are sinners. The following verses clearly back up this fact.

"As it is written, There is none righteous, no, not one."—Rom. 3:10.

"For all have sinned, and come short of the glory of God."—Rom. 3:23.

"For there is not a just man upon earth, that doeth good, and sinneth not."—Eccles. 7:20.

"But we are all as an unclean thing, and all our righteousnesses are as filthy rags; and we all do fade as a leaf; and our iniquities, like the wind, have taken us away."—Isa. 64:6.

Many parents are amazed by the fact that they do not have to teach their children to sin! That is one ability that comes naturally to all men. Sin is not only the action that a person does; it is what he is. We are sinners by nature, and sin is the product of what we are by nature. The only way to understand what makes a man a sinner is to see how sin got on this earth to begin with. The Bible says, *"Wherefore, as by one man sin entered into the world, and death by sin; and so death passed upon all men, for that all have sinned"* (Rom. 5:12).

According to Romans 5:12, sin entered into the world by one man, Adam. According to Genesis 1:27, Adam was made in the image of God; but after his disobedience in the Garden, that image was marred by sin.

Genesis 5:1–3 states, *"This is the book of the generations of Adam. In the day that God created man, in the likeness of God made he him; Male and female created he them; and blessed them, and called their name Adam, in the day when they were created. And Adam lived an hundred and thirty years, and begat a son in his own likeness, after his image; and called his name Seth."*

> Even our best works are corrupted from the source.

God created man in the likeness of Himself, but the Bible clearly refers to Seth in a different light. Seth was not made in God's likeness or image but in the fallen likeness and image of his father, Adam. Like Seth, every human inherits a sin nature, and along with that sin nature we reap the consequences of sin. We are sinners because we are born in sin. We are not sinners because we sin: we sin because we are sinners.

When God said in Isaiah 64:6 that all of man's righteous works are nothing but filthy rags, He reminded us that since we are sinners, the very source of our works, as good as they may be, is still unclean. Even our best works are corrupted from the source. Because of this fact, no man can be saved by his own works.

Sin Separates Man From God

It is not only important to understand the nature of sin but also to understand the consequences of sin. Romans 5:18 says, *"Therefore as by the offence of one judgment came upon all men to condemnation; even so by the righteousness of one the free gift came upon all men unto justification of life."* Because of sin, man is separated from God. Romans 3:23 further explains, *"For all have sinned, and come short of the glory of God."*

The Sinner Is Condemned to Hell

Being a sinner, he is therefore condemned by one man's act.

John 3:18 states, *"He that believeth on him is not condemned: but he that believeth not is condemned already, because he hath not believed in the name of the only begotten Son of God."* Also, John 3:36 tells us, *"He that believeth on the Son hath everlasting life: and he that believeth not the Son shall not see life; but the wrath of God abideth on him."* Romans 6:23 explains, *"The wages of sin is death."* Man's sinful nature separates him from God, and that separation leads to eternal condemnation.

God's Remedy

Thank God, His Gospel is not just a presentation of the darkness of sin. There is a bright ray of hope which He offers to all men. Although Adam's disobedience plunged the entire human race into sin, Jesus Christ's perfect, sinless life provided the acceptable sacrifice that was required to save man from sin. God freely offers the forgiveness of sins through Jesus Christ to all who will receive Him.

It is imperative that the soul winner understand and master the doctrines of Christ and salvation. Religious systems and liberal churches today have invented their own remedies for sin and their own ways to Heaven. Because of these false doctrines, people have replaced God's way (the *only way* to Heaven) with their own way. In some cults, Christ has been blatantly replaced or left out. In one way or another, every major cult today denies Jesus' deity or God's remedy for sin.

"Jesus said unto her, I am the resurrection, and the life: he that believeth in me, though he were dead, yet shall he live: And whosoever liveth and believeth in me shall never die. Believest thou this?"—John 11:25, 26.

"I am the door: by me if any man enter in, he shall be saved, and shall go in and out, and find pasture."—John 10:9.

Every soul winner at one time or another will have to confront the false belief of a cult while defending his own belief in Christ. The Word of God is the only line of defense in these situations. It will never return void, and it will always accomplish the purpose for which God intended it.

The Person of Christ—His Deity

Christ Is Called God

Many cults today deny the fact that Jesus Christ is an equal part of the Trinity. Therefore, it is important that we understand from the Scriptures that Christ is called God. In fact, in Hebrews Christ is called God by the Heavenly Father Himself (Heb. 1:1–8 below).

Each of the following Scriptures clearly indicates and proves the deity of our Lord Jesus Christ:

"God, who at sundry times and in divers manners spake in time past unto the fathers by the prophets, Hath in these last days spoken unto us by his Son, whom he hath appointed heir of all things, by whom also he made the worlds; Who being the brightness of his glory, and the express image of his person, and upholding all things by the word of his power, when he had by himself purged our sins, sat down on the right hand of the Majesty on high; Being made so much better than the angels, as he hath by inheritance obtained a more excellent name than they. For unto which of the angels said he at any time, Thou art my Son, this day have I begotten thee? And again, I will be to him a Father, and he shall be to me a Son? And again, when he bringeth in the firstbegotten into the world, he saith, And let all the angels of God worship him. And of the angels he saith, Who maketh his angels spirits, and his ministers a flame of fire. But unto the Son he saith, **Thy throne, O God, is for ever and ever:** *a sceptre of righteousness is the sceptre of thy kingdom."*— Heb. 1:1–8.

"And Thomas answered and said unto him, **My Lord and my God.** *Jesus saith unto him, Thomas, because thou hast seen me, thou hast believed: blessed are they that have not seen, and yet have believed."*—John 20:28, 29.

"Looking for that blessed hope, and the glorious appearing of **the great God and our** <u>**Saviour Jesus Christ**</u>*."*—Titus 2:13.

"And we know that the Son of God is come, and hath given us an understanding, that we may know him that is true, and we are in him that

*is true, even in his Son Jesus Christ. **This is the true God, and eternal life.***"—I John 5:20.

"*For in him dwelleth all the **fulness of the Godhead bodily.***"—Col. 2:9.

"*And the **Word was made flesh**, and dwelt among us, (and we beheld his glory, the glory as of the only begotten of the Father,) full of grace and truth.*"—John 1:14.

"*Then saith Jesus unto him, Get thee hence, Satan: for it is written, Thou shalt worship the **Lord thy God**, and him only shalt thou serve.*"—Matt. 4:10.

"*Verily, verily, I say unto you, He that heareth my word, and believeth on him that sent me, hath everlasting life, and shall not come into condemnation; but is passed from death unto life. Verily, verily, I say unto you, The hour is coming, and now is, when the dead shall hear the voice of the **Son of God**: and they that hear shall live.*"—John 5:24, 25.

In these verses, Christ was *called God* and *received worship as God*. Anyone who truly believes God's Word cannot deny the deity of Christ.

Pre-Existence

"*In the beginning was the Word, and the Word was with God, and the Word was God.*"—John 1:1.

"*In the beginning God created the heaven and the earth.*"—Gen. 1:1.

"*Jesus said unto them, Verily, verily, I say unto you, Before Abraham was, I am.*"—John 8:58.

"*And this is life eternal, that they might know thee the only true God, and Jesus Christ, whom thou hast sent. I have glorified thee on the earth: I have finished the work which thou gavest me to do. And now, O Father, glorify thou me with thine own self with the glory which I had with thee before the world was.*"—John 17:3–5.

"*Who, being in the form of God, thought it not robbery to be equal with God.*"—Phil. 2:6.

"For by him were all things created, that are in heaven, and that are in earth, visible and invisible, whether they be thrones, or dominions, or principalities, or powers: all things were created by him, and for him."—Col. 1:16.

Self-Existence and Life-Giving Power

"For as the Father raiseth up the dead, and quickeneth them; even so the Son quickeneth whom he will."—John 5:21.

"For as the Father hath life in himself; so hath he given to the Son to have life in himself."—John 5:26.

"In him was life; and the life was the light of men."—John 1:4.

"Who is made, not after the law of a carnal commandment, but after the power of an endless life."—Heb. 7:16.

"And this is life eternal, that they might know thee the only true God, and Jesus Christ, whom thou hast sent. I have glorified thee on the earth: I have finished the work which thou gavest me to do. And now, O Father, glorify thou me with thine own self with the glory which I had with thee before the world was."—John 17:3–5.

Omnipotence

"And Jesus came and spake unto them, saying, All power is given unto me in heaven and in earth."—Matt. 28:18.

"I am he that liveth, and was dead; and, behold, I am alive for evermore, Amen; and have the keys of hell and of death."—Rev. 1:18.

"As thou hast given him power over all flesh, that he should give eternal life to as many as thou hast given him."—John 17:2.

"Which he wrought in Christ, when he raised him from the dead, and set him at his own right hand in the heavenly places, Far above all principality, and power, and might, and dominion, and every name that is named, not only in this world, but also in that which is to come: And hath put all things under his feet, and gave him to be the head over all things to the church."—Eph. 1:20–22.

"Who being the brightness of his glory, and the express image of his person, and upholding all things by the word of his power, when he had by himself purged our sins, sat down on the right hand of the Majesty on high."—Heb. 1:3.

"Thou hast put all things in subjection under his feet. For in that he put all in subjection under him, he left nothing that is not put under him."— Heb. 2:8.

Omniscience

"Now are we sure that thou knowest all things, and needest not that any man should ask thee: by this we believe that thou camest forth from God."— John 16:30.

"But Jesus did not commit himself unto them, because he knew all men."—John 2:24.

"In whom are hid all the treasures of wisdom and knowledge."— Col. 2:3.

"And immediately when Jesus perceived in his spirit that they so reasoned within themselves, he said unto them, Why reason ye these things in your hearts?"—Mark 2:8.

"Nathanael saith unto him, Whence knowest thou me? Jesus answered and said unto him, Before that Philip called thee, when thou wast under the fig tree, I saw thee."—John 1:48.

Omnipresence

"For where two or three are gathered together in my name, there am I in the midst of them."—Matt. 18:20.

"Teaching them to observe all things whatsoever I have commanded you: and, lo, I am with you alway, even unto the end of the world."— Matt. 28:20.

"Which is his body, the fulness of him that filleth all in all."— Eph. 1:23.

These verses show that Jesus Christ possessed the qualities of deity; thus, they prove His deity. In addition, they show the awesome power and purity of God's provision in Christ.

Divine Offices Are Ascribed to Jesus Christ

Creator

"All things were made by him; and without him was not any thing made that was made."—John 1:3.

"And, Thou, Lord, in the beginning hast laid the foundation of the earth; and the heavens are the works of thine hands."—Heb. 1:10.

"For by him were all things created, that are in heaven, and that are in earth, visible and invisible, whether they be thrones, or dominions, or principalities, or powers: all things were created by him, and for him: And he is before all things, and by him all things consist. And he is the head of the body, the church: who is the beginning, the firstborn from the dead; that in all things he might have the preeminence."—Col. 1:16–18.

Power to Forgive Sins

"When Jesus saw their faith, he said unto the sick of the palsy, Son, thy sins be forgiven thee. But there were certain of the scribes sitting there, and reasoning in their hearts, Why doth this man thus speak blasphemies? who can forgive sins but God only? And immediately when Jesus perceived in his spirit that they so reasoned within themselves, he said unto them, Why reason ye these things in your hearts? Whether is it easier to say to the sick of the palsy, Thy sins be forgiven thee; or to say, Arise, and take up thy bed, and walk? But that ye may know that the Son of man hath power on earth to forgive sins, (he saith to the sick of the palsy,) I say unto thee, Arise, and take up thy bed, and go thy way into thine house."—Mark 2:5–11.

"And he said unto her, Thy sins are forgiven."—Luke 7:48.

Power Over Death

"And this is the Father's will which hath sent me, that of all which he hath given me I should lose nothing, but should raise it up again at the last day. And this is the will of him that sent me, that every one which seeth the

Son, and believeth on him, may have everlasting life: and I will raise him up at the last day."—John 6:39, 40.

"Whoso eateth my flesh, and drinketh my blood, hath eternal life; and I will raise him up at the last day."—John 6:54.

"Jesus said unto her, I am the resurrection, and the life: he that believeth in me, though he were dead, yet shall he live."—John 11:25.

The Provision of Christ—His Cross

God's provision for our salvation is found not only in the Person of Jesus Christ but also in His work. Christ's work at Calvary was a work of redemption. As previously shown, there was a need for a Redeemer because of man's sin problem. The following verses can be used to explain and clarify the work of Christ on the cross:

"Forasmuch as ye know that ye were not redeemed with corruptible things, as silver and gold, from your vain conversation received by tradition from your fathers; But with the precious blood of Christ, as of a lamb without blemish and without spot."—I Pet. 1:18, 19.

"But God commendeth his love toward us, in that, while we were yet sinners, Christ died for us."—Rom. 5:8.

"Therefore by the deeds of the law there shall no flesh be justified in his sight: for by the law is the knowledge of sin."—Rom. 3:20.

"The next day John seeth Jesus coming unto him, and saith, Behold the Lamb of God, which taketh away the sin of the world."—John 1:29.

"But if we walk in the light, as he is in the light, we have fellowship one with another, and the blood of Jesus Christ his Son cleanseth us from all sin."—I John 1:7.

"For I delivered unto you first of all that which I also received, how that Christ died for our sins according to the scriptures; And that he was buried, and that he rose again the third day according to the scriptures."—I Cor. 15:3, 4.

Christ's completed work of redemption is summarized in I Corinthians 15:3, 4. This passage explains how Christ was offered up on the cross as the perfect sacrifice. He fulfills the Scriptures, and He fulfills God's righteous demand for the payment of sin by His death, His burial and His resurrection. Christ purchased sinners with His shed blood. He died on the cross and then rose from the grave victoriously. Now He makes intercession for us in Heaven.

> Satan has helped man devise hundreds of supposed ways to gain salvation that are contrary to the Bible.

Thank God for His provision! Some minimize the blood atonement today and call *the blood* a mere symbol of death. However, the Word of God declares, *"...without shedding of blood is no remission"* (Heb. 9:22).

It is important to remember that God gave only one provision for man's sin problem. He is Jesus Christ, the Redeemer, whom He had promised to send. That remedy was and still is receiving Jesus Christ as Saviour and accepting His death on the cross as payment in full for your sins. Acts 4:12 confirms this: *"Neither is there salvation in any other: for there is none other name under heaven given among men, whereby we must be saved."*

It has been stated that for everything God has given to man, Satan has made a counterfeit. In the area of salvation, Satan has helped man devise hundreds of supposed ways to gain salvation that are contrary to the Bible. Men would like to believe that they have the power to save themselves, but the Scriptures plainly teach that salvation is found through Jesus Christ alone. Some examples of today's manmade erroneous solutions for sin are:

Baptism • Church attendance • Communion • Confessions • Confirmation • Faithfulness • Feelings • Golden Rule • Good works • Penance • Positive thinking • Promises • Religious experiences • Resolutions • Sacraments • Speaking in tongues • Service • Sacrifice • Ten Commandments • Tithing • Vows

God has one solution for the problem of sin. This solution is the finished work at Calvary by Jesus Christ. Good beliefs and good practices do not save anyone. One's faith must be in *Jesus Christ alone* for salvation.

Many people are trusting in good works for salvation. These people are missing God's free gift, and for those who reject the gift of Jesus Christ, the tragic result is spiritual death. *"For the wages of sin is death; but the gift of God is eternal life through Jesus Christ our Lord"* (Rom. 6:23).

There are millions today who need to hear of God's precious gift. They need to know there is a remedy for sin. Soul winners must fervently declare the *simple* truth of the Gospel. They must spread the good news that the gift of God is eternal life through Jesus Christ our Lord.

Man's Choice

Man's problem of sin and God's remedy for sin through Jesus Christ are the first two aspects of the Gospel, but man's problem will only be solved if he makes the choice to accept God's remedy by faith.

Understanding the Gospel

Before a man can be saved, he must first fully understand that he is a sinner in need of a Saviour. This understanding is necessary if he is to repent before God and accept Christ as Saviour by faith. Note the order of Paul's testimony in Acts 20:21: *"Testifying both to the Jews, and also to the Greeks, **repentance** toward God, and **faith** toward our Lord Jesus Christ."* In the realm of salvation there is a close relationship between repentance and faith. They go hand in hand.

First, *repentance* means to turn around and go in the opposite direction, or to change one's mind. A man repents when he realizes that he is a sinner before God, that he deserves God's righteous judgment, and that he can do nothing to save himself. In this instant, he has changed his mind about his hope of salvation. Second, *faith* is turning to and trusting in Jesus Christ. Faith is believing that Jesus Christ is the only means by which to be forgiven and to receive eternal life.

Repentance and faith cannot be separated; they work together in the single action of turning from self-effort and trusting in Jesus Christ as Saviour. When a man trusts God, he first confesses himself a sinner in need of salvation and then acknowledges his understanding of God's remedy for him through the Gospel. By placing his trust in Christ alone for his salvation, by that very decision, he has repented, and by such faith he is saved.

Exercising Genuine Faith

It is entirely possible for a person to know that he is a sinner and that Christ died for his sins yet still not be saved. A simple head knowledge of the Gospel does not save a person from his sin, nor does it give him the hope of eternal life.

"But without faith it is impossible to please him."—Heb. 11:6.

Genuine faith is claiming, by personal choice, God's promises and is relying exclusively upon Christ's work on the cross to be the sufficient payment for sin.

When a man will admit or confess that he is a sinner in need of a Saviour and will accept Christ by faith, he will be saved. The element of faith is pleasing to God.

First, genuine faith involves choice. Every individual must choose whether to accept or to reject Christ. No one will be in Heaven because he grew up in church or because his grandpa was a Baptist preacher. Each citizen of Heaven will be a citizen by choice.

"But as many as received him, to them gave he power to become the sons of God, even to them that believe on his name: Which were born, not of blood, nor of the will of the flesh, nor of the will of man, but of God."—John 1:12, 13.

Second, faith involves trust. When a person believes the Gospel, he must rely entirely upon Jesus Christ for salvation. There is no room for trusting in anything other than Christ. Faith involves *trusting, relying, grasping, claiming, seizing* and *believing*. Each of these words involves taking possession of something. All of these actions take place when faith is placed in Jesus Christ.

It is history when one says, "Christ died on Calvary." It is theology when one says, "Christ died on Calvary for the sins of mankind." It is salvation when one can say, "Christ died on Calvary for my sins, and I have accepted Him as my personal Saviour."

Recently I was witnessing to a dear couple with a Roman Catholic background. As I presented the Gospel to them, I sensed that they were willing to pray to Jesus Christ, yet they still had a desire to look to the Catholic Church as a part of their salvation. I stood on their stairway as I gave them an illustration of salvation. I told them to imagine that there was a fire upstairs and that outside the window there were firemen holding a net for them to jump into to be saved. I explained to them that in order to be saved from the fire in the house, they would have to let go totally of their faith in the house for protection and safety and completely trust the firemen. I encouraged the couple to release completely their trust in a church and to rely entirely on Jesus Christ for their salvation.

Within a few moments, they both prayed and accepted Christ alone for their salvation! Genuine faith involves trust in Christ alone.

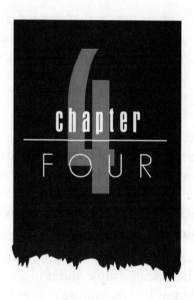

Presenting

the Gospel

"For God so loved the world, that he gave his only begotten Son, that whosoever believeth in him should not perish, but have everlasting life."—John 3:16.

We now come to the heart of the book. Jesus came "to seek and to save," and we are to carry out His commission by presenting His Gospel in this day. The soul winner's duty is to master the plan of salvation presented in the Bible and then allow the Holy Spirit to be in complete control of what he actually says.

A gospel presentation should never be lacking a basic plan or structure to keep it as clear, simple and understandable as possible. A good plan will aid us in overcoming our own human limitations while allowing the Holy Spirit complete freedom to do His work as well. In my own soul-winning ministry, I have always used a general framework for presenting the Gospel, but many times the Holy Spirit has prompted me to take a completely different approach.

Several different methods have been helpful to my efforts in soul winning as well as the efforts of many other fruitful soul winners in the past. While considering these proven methods, the soul winner should remember never to become dependent on man's ideas on what to say at a given time. He should completely rely on the Holy Spirit's leading. In verses 22 and 23 of Jude's epistle, the Bible states, *"And of some have compassion, making a difference: And others save with fear, pulling them out of the fire; hating even the garment spotted by the flesh."* In this passage, God's Word clearly teaches the saints that different people will be won to Christ by different approaches. Some will respond to a message of compassion, while others will have to be won by a message of fear regarding their eternal destiny without Christ. We may not understand which message is necessary at which time. That uncertainty is why prayer and the leading of the Holy Spirit are so necessary in soul winning.

The Introduction, the First Few Words

A soul winner should never underestimate the significance of the opening words of each visit. These initial words of conversation on a visit determine the lasting impression that the prospect will carry throughout that visit. They can immediately turn the person away or, on the other hand, put the person at ease if they are spoken carefully and are Spirit-led. Prior to knocking on one door, every soul-winning team should pray for God's control.

Introducing Yourself

Depending on the type of soul-winning call, your introduction will vary. The introduction for a *contact* call (a special visit made only to a person who has had some sort of direct or indirect contact with the church) is different from the introduction for a door-to-door or random soul-winning approach. Regardless of the type of visit, the soul winner should approach the door in a spirit of optimism and expectation.

A sample opening statement for a *contact* soul-winning call is found below. As previously stated, the introduction for *door-to-door* soul winning will, of course, vary somewhat from this pattern; however, many of these opening statements are applicable to a *door-to-door* situation as well.

> *Mr. Jones? Hello, my name is..., and this is.... We are from...Baptist Church. We are happy to have Joey as a part of our children's Sunday school class. We would love to be able to take a few minutes and tell you a little about our Sunday school program. Could you spare a few moments for us to tell you a few things about the program?*

Although there are several types of soul-winning situations, there are five elements that should be part of every soul-winning introduction:

1. *Find out the prospect's name and then use it.*
2. *Communicate your own name clearly as well as your partner's*

name. Use of personal names puts the visit on a personal level.)

3. *State the name of the church clearly. (Being from a Baptist church may relieve the person's fear of cult association.)*
4. *State the reason for the visit.*
5. *Ask the listener for a few moments of his time.*

Starting the Conversation

After the introduction, there is usually a need to talk casually for a moment. Normally, a few minutes of general conversation pave the way for the soul winner to present the Gospel.

Every soul winner needs to be genuinely interested in people and in their lives. Because of this genuine interest, certain questions can be asked that express genuine concern. At the beginning of the conversation, relevant questions might deal with how long they have lived in their house, a trophy on a shelf, or some other conversational topic. *The soul winner should encourage the person to talk, and in turn he should learn to listen.*

Continuing the Conversation

Though he may begin the conversation a bit trivially, the soul winner should lead the discussion toward spiritual things. At some point in the conversation, the soul winner must find out the person's religious background, as well as present the ministry of the church. Learning the religious background is important for gaining an understanding of the person's spiritual condition. While visiting the parents of a child on a bus route, a soul winner might learn this by asking, "Did you ever attend Sunday school like Bobby?" As a person reveals his religious background, the soul winner must be careful not to criticize or jump to quick conclusions. Rather, he should listen intently and remember details of the person's background to help later in the discussion. If the prospect attended a Catholic school, for example, appropriate Scriptures can be utilized *later* in the visit.

Continuing on in the discussion, one or more of questions may be helpful with Bobby's parents: "How hear about the church?" "Do you have any questions a class?" "Do you know why we have a Sunday school Questions like these can help provide a very smooth transition to the gospel plan of salvation.

Though the introduction and initial conversation in any visit are crucial, a soul winner should not spend more than five to ten minutes on the introductory remarks. We do not know how much time God will give us at that address; therefore, it is important that we transfer the conversation to the Gospel. After covering some common ground with the individual, the soul winner should be ready to present the Gospel.

Turning the Conversation Toward Christ

After laying this introductory groundwork with the individual, the Spirit will reveal the proper time to transfer the conversation from the generalities of church and religion to the specific truth of Christ. At this crucial time of transition, I have found three general sentence ideas to be effective.

> **Statement 1:** *"Mr. Jones, I think it is really good that you are sending your child to Sunday school, and I am also glad to know that you have a religious background."*

> **Statement 2:** *"It is very important that each of us attends church and that our children attend Sunday school. I have always enjoyed church attendance."*

> **Statement 3:** *"However, church attendance and religion in themselves have never given salvation to anyone."*

These three pivotal statements are called the "three Cs." The soul winner has just *complimented* the individual for his past church involvement; he has *compared himself* to the individual; and he has *corrected* any erroneous thought that religion can save someone.

At this point, a *brief personal testimony* by the soul winner is

The Three Cs

Compliment

Compare

Correct

often helpful. This testimony should reaffirm the three Cs: *compliment, compare* and *correct*. The testimony should tell of the soul winner's condition before being saved and of his discovery that religion could not save him. It should also include how he heard of God's plan of salvation and how he accepted Christ. In the conclusion of the testimony, he should *state that he is sure that he is on his way to Heaven* and that Christ has made a wonderful difference in his life.

Two Important Questions

At this point in the visit, the soul winner has talked about the church and also about the prospect's religious background and perhaps even shared his own testimony. Now it is time to begin the process of leading the person to Christ. *This process is begun by asking two very important questions.*

The first question turns the focus from the soul winner's life to the individual. I personally might say it this way: "I have been telling you about my background. Now, what about you? Are you sure that when this life is over, you will spend eternity in Heaven?"

Normally, the person will respond with a simple "yes" or "no" to this question. If the person says "no," then the soul winner can ask him if he may share with him a few Scriptures which describe God's plan of salvation. It is wise at this point for the soul winner to reaffirm that he is not teaching denominational facts but rather that he is simply sharing from God's Word. If the person says, "Yes, I would go to Heaven," or "I think so," the soul winner will want to ask him, "How do you know that you are on your way to Heaven?"

The average semi-religious unsaved man would respond to that question by explaining that he believes in God in some general way. At this point the soul winner should agree that it is important to believe in God and then ask if he may show him what the Bible says (not what some preacher's or teacher's opinion is) about how a person can be sure that he is on his way to Heaven. Most people are placing their hopes in false beliefs for eternal life. Soul winners have the responsibility of sharing from the Bible the truth of salvation through Christ alone.

The Heart of the Message

These preliminary statements and questions may seem repetitious and unnecessary to some; however, they are vital in preparing for the next phase of the call, the *heart of the message*. Reaching souls for Christ is the purpose for which the soul winner has made great preparation and study. Reaching souls for Christ can only be accomplished by the presentation of the gospel plan of salvation. This is the heart of the message. The specific goal for each soul-winning call is to present God's simple plan of salvation to the prospect and to encourage him to accept Christ as his personal Saviour. This is why we use the term "soul winning," not "church visitation program." Each visit should be viewed as a soul-winning opportunity!

When God opens the opportunity to present the gospel plan of salvation, each soul winner must ask the Holy Spirit to give him the scriptural pattern that is pleasing to the Lord and that is most effective for each individual person. There are hundreds of verses which directly relate to man's salvation. However, it is not necessary to teach the prospect a course on the doctrine of soteriology. The goal is to lead him to trust Christ as Saviour without delay!

A Suggested Approach

Some soul winners will use a gospel tract as a guide during this part of the soul winning call, but the soul winner's final authority must be the Bible itself. When the prospect actually reads the verse himself, he comprehends it better; therefore, the Word will have a greater impact on his conscience. The following is the basic framework of God's wonderful plan of salvation, along with the Bible verses which should be read by the prospect throughout the scriptural presentation of the Gospel.

Realize that there is none good.

"As it is written, There is none righteous, no, not one."—
Rom. 3:10.

See yourself as a sinner.

"For all have sinned, and come short of the glory of God."—
Rom. 3:23.

After reading these two verses, it would be wise to explain that all men have a sin nature and that sin separates them from God and from His glory. Romans 5:12 can also be used at this point: *"Wherefore, as by one man sin entered into the world, and death by sin; and so death passed upon all men, for that all have sinned."* This verse is especially helpful if the person has a religious background with a basic knowledge of Adam and Eve. However, in recent years, America has become increasingly pagan, and many young people have never learned about Adam.

Notice God's price on sin.

"For the wages of sin is death; but the gift of God is eternal life through Jesus Christ our Lord."—Rom. 6:23.

Realize that Christ died for you.

"But God commendeth his love toward us, in that, while we were yet sinners, Christ died for us."—Rom. 5:8.

Use an illustration of the words *wages* and *gift* to depict the meaning of Romans 6:23. *Wage* can be defined as a "deserving payment." An illustration would be that even as a man deserves his paycheck as payment for his work, so man deserves spiritual death as payment for his sin. Review quickly Romans 3:23 and return to Romans 6:23 to reaffirm that all have sinned and that the wages of sin is death.

The concept of a gift can be illustrated by relating it to a birthday or Christmas gift. The soul winner can explain that a gift which is received has already been paid for. It should also be explained to the prospect that Christian salvation is something that has already been paid for by the death of Jesus Christ on the cross. Just as in receiving a physical gift, one needs only to accept salvation as a free gift paid for by the shed blood of Jesus Christ.

Next, the soul winner should turn to Romans 10 to show how a person may receive this gift of salvation. The Scriptures mandate that a person must believe in his heart to be saved.

Claim salvation.

"That if thou shalt confess with thy mouth the Lord Jesus, and shalt believe in thine heart that God hath raised him from the dead, thou shalt be saved. For with the heart man believeth unto righteousness; and with the mouth confession is made unto salvation. For the scripture saith, Whosoever believeth on him shall not be ashamed."—Rom. 10:9–11.

NOTE: John 3:16 may also be used at this time: *"For God so loved the world, that he gave his only begotten Son, that whosoever believeth in him should not perish, but have everlasting life."*

Take God at His Word.

"For whosoever shall call upon the name of the Lord shall be saved."—Rom. 10:13.

After reading these Scriptures, there is now an opportunity to explain to the prospect that anyone who believes that he is a sinner and that Jesus Christ, God's Son, died and rose again for him, may pray and receive Christ and His salvation. It is good to stress **confessing with their mouth** as well as **believing in their heart**. Certainly prayer without faith cannot save; however, confession or prayer with the mouth should be the natural manifestation of true belief in the heart. Therefore, when reading Romans 10:9–11, the soul winner should show not only the importance of belief but also the importance of expressing that belief. This need for praying or "confessing" should be emphasized during the presentation of the Gospel in order to prepare the prospect to pray and to express his faith in Jesus Christ.

After reading and explaining God's plan of salvation, the soul winner will want to review these three basic principles with his soul-winning prospect: 1) that all men are sinners and that sin separates men from God, 2) that Jesus died to forgive men's sins, and 3) that if one will admit his need for Christ (because of sin) and will place his trust in Him alone for salvation, he will be saved.

If the individual understands and believes the Gospel, the soul winner may, at this point, encourage the individual to pray and accept Jesus Christ as Saviour. Before encouraging any prospect to pray, however, the soul winner needs to be sure that the prospect has *completely understood* the Scriptures covered.

Leading to a Decision

After the introductory remarks and the gospel presentation have been completed, it is time to encourage the soul-winning prospect to accept Christ. This is the most exciting part of the soul-winning call. As with the other aspects of the call, presenting the need to make a decision for Christ should be done in an orderly manner.

When encouraging the prospect to pray and to receive Christ, three effective questions are as follows:

> *"Mr. Jones, do you believe that you are a sinner, separated from God, and without the ability to save yourself?"*
>
> *"Do you believe that Jesus, God's Son, shed His blood to pay for your sin?"*
>
> *"Would there be anything that would stop you from praying and accepting Jesus Christ as your Saviour today?"*

Often the answer to the first two questions is "yes." The answer to the third question in most cases will be "no." However, a person may not want to pray and receive Christ because of fear or uncertainty. To address a prospect who expresses fear, the soul winner may explain with encouragement that he also was fearful at first when making this important decision but is now thankful to have made it.

After sharing the Gospel, keep all potential lines of communication open.

When a person digs in and becomes determined not to make a decision for Christ or to listen any further, the soul winner should leave a gospel tract with his phone number on it. He should make the prospect feel welcome to call his own home when he is ready to accept Christ or if he has any questions at all about salvation. With a willing prospect, the soul winner should then try his best to set up another visit and then politely leave the prospect with prayers that the Holy Spirit will continue His work.

Periodically a person will call the person who visited him shortly after that initial visit because the Holy Spirit would not allow him to stop thinking about the visit. Anyone who has listened to the complete gospel presentation could become ready to receive Christ at any time; therefore, the soul winner should keep all potential lines of communication open.

When a prospect agrees that there is nothing that would stand in the way of his praying and receiving Christ, Romans 10:9, 10 and 13 should be reviewed with him. The grace of God by which we are saved is extended to those who have a genuine belief in the heart. That should be followed by open confession with the mouth. Matthew 10:32 explains, *"Whosoever therefore shall confess me before men, him will I confess also before my Father which is in heaven." "For with the heart man believeth unto righteousness; and with the mouth confession is made unto salvation"* (Rom. 10:10).

Most of the time if the person is ready to make the decision, he will still be a bit hesitant about praying, especially out loud. Usually it is because of the fact that he does not really know how to pray. But if the Gospel is thoroughly and properly presented and the prospect understands and believes the truth, there is no reason why he cannot pray his own prayer to accept Jesus Christ as Saviour.

If the person truly believes and understands the truth of the Gospel, he should be able to express that belief verbally. True, he might feel awkward, but he should at least attempt to pray on his own. It is all right to suggest the contents of a prayer, but a soul winner should be careful about always encouraging people to repeat his prayer. Confession for salvation is a personal decision. Many times a few words of instruction in what prayer is or maybe an initial prayer by the soul winner will relieve any inhibitions.

While the truth of the Gospel is simple to understand, one must try not to oversimplify the process of confession. In some cases, it may be helpful to have a prospect repeat a prayer, especially if English is his second language; however, even in this case, the soul winner should encourage the prospect to pray his own prayer of confession of his trust in Christ. Confession is never easy, but when a person confesses his belief in Christ as Saviour, he will remember the day the decision was made, and he will never be trusting in some "magical prayer" to save him from his sins.

After *thoroughly* covering the need to pray and to accept Christ, the soul winner may say, "Mr. Jones, I would like to encourage you to pray and ask Christ to forgive your sins and become your Saviour."

If the prospect is hesitant, the soul winner should immediately again encourage the prospect to pray. The soul winner should also assure the prospect by telling him that he would also like to pray for him once he has received Christ as his Saviour.

At this point, Lord willing, you will hear the most beautiful sound ever heard. That is the sound of a sinner saying in his own words a prayer for salvation. At the conclusion of the prayer, you will want to pray a prayer of thankgiving to the Lord for the wonderful decision. You should be ready to pray as soon as the person stops praying. Remember, a person may not end his prayer by saying "Amen."

Mike Anderson was a vice president with the bank our church had done business with over a period of years. I remember first meeting Mike and discussing some of the desires and goals of the church with him. As I shared our vision of the church with Mike, I sensed that he was curious as to how a group of people could go forward in such a way and do a work for God by faith. At that point, I stopped and shared with him my personal testimony of salvation and the joy of knowing that one day I would spend eternity with the Lord in Heaven. I shared with Mike that the Gospel is the sole purpose for all of the vision for the church expansion that I had shared with

> The moment an individual accepts Christ, Satan will begin to bring doubt and discouragement.

him. Over years of doing business with Mike, I had several opportunities to share the Gospel with him, but something always seemed to interrupt the message at the point of decision. Nevertheless, I continued to put gospel materials into his hands through the mail.

Finally, a day came when Mike visited my office. It was a quiet afternoon, about 5:00 p.m., and the Lord laid on my heart to ask Mike if he had been thinking about some of the materials I had sent him in the mail. He said he had been, and I asked him if he knew for sure that when this life was over he would spend eternity in Heaven. Although Mike was a moral man with a religious background, he said to me in an honest way, "I'm not sure I would spend eternity in Heaven." I then asked Mike if I could share with him some verses which would give him the confidence that he would one day be with the Lord. He said yes, and I basically followed the plan which has been presented to you in this chapter.

I will never forget the joy of hearing this man, now in his fifties, bow his head and humbly confess to the Lord that he was a sinner, unable to save himself, and ask Christ to come into his life and save him!

There are many who say that old-fashioned, one-on-one soul winning is a thing of the past, but I thank God for the way He continues to use people like you and me to share this wonderful story with a lost and dying world.

Leaving a New Christian With Confidence

The moment an individual accepts Christ as his personal Saviour, Satan will begin to bring doubt and discouragement into his life. The soul winner must give this person scriptural support and encouragement to solidify his faith in the Lord. Although more assurance verses will be shared on a later follow-up visit, it is good to share a few verses before leaving a new Christian.

Often it is good to read I John 5:11–13: *"And this is the record, that God hath given to us eternal life, and this life is in his Son. He that hath the Son hath life; and he that hath not the Son of God hath not* *life. These things have I written unto you that believe on the name of the Son of God; that ye may **know** that ye have eternal life, and that ye may believe on the name of the Son of God."*

After reading these verses, the soul winner may ask the new Christian, "Based upon the Scriptures, if your life ended today, where would you spend eternity?" He should respond with a smile, "Heaven!"

A close look at the Great Commission will reveal that the soul winner should not only be concerned with teaching the truth of salvation but also with seeing the new Christian baptized. The job of a soul winner does not end there. The soul winner should ensure that the new Christian is being thoroughly trained in God's Word so that he can mature in his Christian walk.

Once the new convert has prayed a prayer of salvation, the soul winner should not breathe a sigh of relief, pat the new Christian on the back, and walk out of the home. Everything possible needs to be done to make sure that this person has assurance of his salvation. He simply needs to be left with one or two Scriptures which explain that if he has sincerely accepted Christ as Saviour, he can know that he is saved. No one should be left with a false assurance, nor should anyone be convinced that he is saved if he has not made a sincere decision.

There are many other Scriptures which teach the assurance of salvation; however, I John 5:11–13 is clear and helpful to use before leaving the home. If there is still some question, Ephesians 2:8, 9, John 1:12 or John 3:3–7 may be helpful.

One of Satan's greatest tricks with these "babes in Christ" is to send his "false teachers" to confuse them. They grab hold of new Christians like leeches and begin to misdirect them. These false teachers will convince new Christians that they are not saved until they speak in tongues. Others may teach that Joseph Smith was inspired of God and that the Mormon church is the only way to Heaven. Many more books could be filled with

> The job of a soul winner does not end when a soul is saved... in fact...it has just begun.

warnings concerning these false teachers and their doctrines.

Colossians 2:6–8 says, *"As ye have therefore received Christ Jesus the Lord, so walk ye in him: Rooted and built up in him, and stablished in the faith, as ye have been taught, abounding therein with thanksgiving. Beware lest any man spoil you through philosophy and vain deceit, after the tradition of men, after the rudiments of the world, and not after Christ."* With this thought in mind, the soul winner must immediately help this new Christian by giving him Scriptures and teaching that will provide him with assurance of his salvation. In most cases, this requires regular and conscientious follow-up with the person.

One final suggestion concerning assurance of salvation is that each soul winner should write down the date of the new convert's salvation in the new convert's Bible or on a gospel tract. The soul winner may want to explain to the new Christian that this is his spiritual birthday and that he does not ever have to doubt his salvation because he has the promise of the Word of God that, because he believed on Jesus Christ as his Saviour on such-and-such a date, he has everlasting life (John 5:24).

It has been my joy to write down the date of salvation for many people. Several years ago I was preaching at a church in northern California. A man came to me, opened his wallet and showed me a gospel tract. On the tract was written, "9-15-83, your salvation day!" He said, "You wrote that the day you led me to Christ!" Times like these are the blessings that God gives to remind us that the work we do for Him is making a difference for eternity. Thank God for the privilege of serving Him!

chapter

FIVE

Procedures

in soul winning

"Now then we are ambassadors for Christ."—II Cor. 5:20.

Although a knowledge of the Scriptures and a planned approach to presenting the Gospel are two definite prerequisites for the prepared soul winner, the soul winner must also possess proper manners and etiquette for soul winning. These physical aspects of soul winning are very important mainly for the purpose of presenting a good testimony for Christ. While it is not our intention to overemphasize outward appearance, manner and appearance are especially vital in the organized soul-winning program. The most important area of soul winning is always the preparation of the heart. The Bible never indicates that only the good-looking, best-dressed people can be used of God to win souls. To the contrary, the Scriptures are full of examples where God has greatly used the "foolish things of the world to confound the wise."

The Bible says in II Corinthians 5:20, "Now then we are ambassadors for Christ." Since every soul winner is an ambassador or representative for Christ, he must keep a proper testimony at all times. He is also an ambassador for his local church and must never forget to represent his church faithfully and unashamedly. There have been many instances in which an ill-mannered soul winner has brought reproach to the name of Christ and to his church. The purpose of this chapter is to give the soul winner the tools necessary to avoid actions that would misrepresent the cause of Christ.

Manners

A basic understanding of proper manners is essential for every soul winner. A soul winner's good manners start with his general testimony to the public. For example, a soul winner should never cut across a yard. He should always use the sidewalk! When knocking on a door, a soul winner should observe which way the door will open and stand on the proper side, so that when the door is opened, the soul winner speaking is the one whom the resident sees first. He should give a polite, clear introduction of himself, his partner and his church. He should avoid getting too close to the resident, respecting that individual's "personal zone" and remembering that he is at that one's home. He should never seek to enter the home of a person who is eating or who is in bedclothes. When talking, he should slow down and be patient in order to avoid interrupting the prospect in the middle of a statement. Although soul winning is by its very nature confrontational, the soul winner has no grounds for being rude or argumentative in his approach.

Compassionate Confrontation

Soul winning is certainly confrontational, but it should not involve a prideful spirit or criticism of a person. The soul winner must possess a compassionate heart. *"He that goeth forth and weepeth, bearing precious seed, shall doubtless come again with rejoicing, bringing his sheaves with him"* (Ps. 126:6).

Not only are the soul winner's manners important, but his partner's manners are important as well. It is imperative that the soul-winning companion be supportive of the soul winner in several areas. First, he should remain interested in what the soul winner is saying and be prepared to offer input if asked. Second, he should aid in minimizing distraction. (Many times the partner can be helpful in quieting children as they get restless.) Last, yet most important of all, a partner should dedicate himself to praying. A partner's prayers can go a long way in winning the spiritual battle for the prospect's soul.

As I was working my way through Bible college, I worked at the Caterpillar Tractor Company one year. I remember one particular spring afternoon when a man from our headquarters walked into the parts department. I was there alone that day, and business was unusually slow. I began to talk with this man named Ray. We discussed tractors, the economy and politics, but I never once mentioned the name of Jesus. You see, I had decided when I started the job that I would spend several months showing a good testimony before I began winning souls. After about an hour of talking with Ray, he walked out to his car and drove back to our headquarters. I thought to myself, *The next time I see Ray, I am going to witness to him.* A few days later we received a memo which stated, "Ray _____, who has been suffering with leukemia," passed away unexpectedly last night." I never had another chance to witness to him because of my own lack of courage. I was afraid to confront a man compassionately with the Gospel of Christ. Though I was a Bible college student, I was not a soul winner. Remember, manners and testimony are important, but they should never be used as an excuse to shirk any opportunity that God gives us to witness.

> Confrontation should never involve a prideful spirit or criticism of a person.

Philosophy of Appearance

A Christian must always remember that he is representing Christ daily. Since the unsaved world cannot look at a Christian's inward spiritual condition, it is imperative that his outward appearance is becoming of a Christian. Paul wrote in II Corinthians 5:17, *"Therefore if any man be in Christ, he is a new creature: old things are passed away; behold, all things are become new."* One must also remember that he has been bought with a price and that he is to glorify God with his appearance.

A few years ago, I was in the home of a man, and I was attempting to present the Gospel to him. This fellow had long hair down to the middle of his back, and he was clothed in black leather and chains. Though his outward appearance seemed rough, the Holy Spirit softened his heart, and he was saved. The next Sunday, a man walked into my Sunday school class who looked vaguely familiar. When I asked him his name he said, "You know me. I'm Dave. You told me how to be saved last Tuesday." I told him that he looked sharp. He then replied by saying, "I just felt so good on the inside, I wanted the outside to match!" What a blessing! Truly, the Holy Spirit teaches a Christian about the importance of being a new creature in Christ.

A good philosophy is that a soul winner's outward appearance should reflect the holiness of God as he follows Jesus Christ as his example. *"For even hereunto were ye called: because Christ also suffered for us, leaving us an example, that ye should follow his steps"* (I Pet. 2:21). Unfortunately, this is not the philosophy of all Christians.

I have noticed several Christian bookstores selling "heavy-metal Christian music" with the singers dressed in leather and chains. When I asked the store manager why, he stated that the philosophy of many "Christians" is that they can reach young people by coming down to their level. Dozens of teenagers were purchasing the tapes and CDs, which served as an incentive for the manager to continue selling them. That kind of philosophy is exactly what the Apostle Paul was addressing when he said,

*"I beseech you therefore, brethren, by the mercies of God, that ye present your bodies a living sacrifice, holy, acceptable unto God, which is your reasonable service. And **be not conformed to this world**: but be ye transformed by the renewing of your mind, that ye may prove what is that good, and acceptable, and perfect, will of God."*—Rom. 12:1, 2.

A Christian will never have to emulate the world in order to win the world. Jesus wants to save people from the world, not call them back into the world!

Practical Tips for Appearance

As stated previously, a soul winner should be trying to present the Gospel as often as possible. Because of that, soul-winning efforts should not be limited to only the times when you are in a shirt and tie. For example, if a person works at a construction site and is wearing blue jeans and a T-shirt when an opportunity to witness comes, he should seize the opportunity.

A soul winner does not have to be dressed up to win a soul to Christ. However, when the soul winners come together for organized church programs, they should dress appropriately to go out and represent their local church and their Lord. Many churches have actual dress requirements for their soul winners to ensure that the appearance of the soul winner is proper.

Being fashionable is not as important as looking clean and sharp when going out. Clothing should be pressed and clean, and colors should match. Appropriate clothing for ladies includes a knee-length skirt or dress with nylons. A woman's clothes should never be tight or clingy, attracting attention to any part of her other than her eyes. For the men, the hair should be cut (above the ear) and combed properly, and shoes should always be shined. A tie, sport coat and dress shoes are appropriate for men in an organized program.

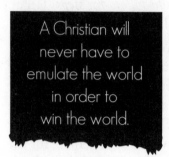

A Christian will never have to emulate the world in order to win the world.

Three key words to remember in regard to appearance are *modesty, neatness* and *appropriateness*. A soul winner should look his best and act with good manners as he represents the Lord!

Vocabulary in Soul Winning

Prior to the 1970s, most Americans were familiar with Biblical terminology, and some were even acquainted with much of the language used by Christians. However, with America's departure from Biblical principles and its overall decline in church attendance, most people are not even remotely familiar with the Bible vocabulary that active Christians use on a daily basis. And since the 1970s, the country has experienced a great influx of immigrants who couple this lack of Biblical knowledge with language difficulty. With these obstacles in mind, a soul winner must be careful not to confuse prospects with terminology that they will not understand. This is another area where the soul winner must depend on the leading of the Holy Spirit to give him the right words to lead souls to Christ.

Many terms which are used frequently in the church will only cause confusion if they are used in a soul-winning call. Rather than saying, "We're out soul winning tonight," it is recommended to say, "We're out visiting," or "We're out telling others about Jesus Christ." Instead of asking, "Has anyone ever told you how to be saved?" it is better to ask, "Has anyone ever told you how to accept Christ as your personal Saviour and know that you are on your way to Heaven?" In no way do these recommendations suggest that a soul winner should "water down" the truth of the Gospel but rather that he use common sense in soul winning.

When encountering someone who *is* familiar with Biblical and church vocabulary, the soul winner should ask questions to make sure that his doctrine of salvation is based on faith in Christ. This person may have grown up in church or may have spent many hours watching religious programs on television. Consequently, he knows all the "language," but he may have never truly accepted Christ as his Saviour. Many times people will appear to be Christians because they know the correct words, but they will often not admit that they are sinners in need of a Saviour.

There are numerous words and phrases which many "religious but lost" people have heard. The wise soul winner will be selective in using the proper substitute words. The question, "Have you ever been born again?" should be replaced with, "Have you ever recognized that you were separated from God and received Jesus Christ as your Saviour?" Rather than asking, "Have you ever trusted Christ?" "Are you a Christian?" "Have you ever trusted God?" or "Have you ever gone forward in church?" it is better to ask, "Are you sure that you are on your way to Heaven?"

Most people are not even remotely familiar with the vocabulary of the Bible.

The alert soul winner must try to determine the depth of the prospect's familiarity with Christian terms and then make the proper adjustments in his speed, delivery and choice of content while presenting the Gospel. We must be discerning teachers who try to understand the level of a prospect's understanding *before* we get too far along with our presentation.

The Soul-Winning Partner

When Christ sent out the first soul winners, He sent them two by two. Besides the fact that it is Biblical, there are many important reasons for going in twos, and there are several functions which a partner can accomplish. The support of a partner can become one of the most important aspects of the visit. He provides accountability, credibility, support, encouragement, companionship, safety and protection against wickedness or slander.

Having a regular soul-winning partner will help a person remain faithful, because he is accountable to another person. If he does not show up at the regular soul-winning time, his partner will be left without someone with whom to go calling. Thus, a soul winner needs to be faithful for his own spiritual benefit, for the benefit of those to whom he will witness, and for his partner's benefit.

> The support of a partner can become one of the most important aspects of the visit.

The faithful soul-winning partner is a tremendous source of support. He is able to fellowship with and encourage the soul winner concerning the importance of spreading the Gospel. Being able to share the victories and defeats with another person creates wonderful memories which may later serve as a great source of encouragement and fellowship.

The Devil will use any trick in the book to ruin a faithful servant of Christ. The person who goes soul winning alone may be setting himself up for trouble. Many men have been the recipients of false accusations by apartment managers, scandalous women or other men who are wicked. A partner's presence can curtail many of these potential problems.

In every area of life, there is a need for leadership and direction. In relation to the soul-winning call, there must be one person doing most of the talking. If two people are attempting to dominate the direction of the conversation, the prospect will be lost in confusion. Many times a soul-winning partner will interrupt with a thought and break the continuity of the presentation. To prevent these situations, the partners should decide before each house which one will do the talking and which one will be the "silent partner." The partner might be a person in training, or he may be an experienced soul winner. In either case, he must allow the other person to dominate the conversation. There may be occasions for the silent partner to speak briefly, but he must be careful not to detract from the gospel plan of salvation. If the soul-winning partner's spiritual background is more similar to the prospect's, it may be helpful for him to share his testimony before the leader for the night shares the gospel presentation.

The greatest help the soul-winning partner can offer is to pray that the Holy Spirit would do a work in the heart of the prospect. *"The effectual fervent prayer of a righteous man availeth much"* (Jas. 5:16). The soul-winning partner should pray continuously before and during each call. He can talk to the Lord while the other partner talks to the prospect.

During the course of a soul-winning call, Satan will send many distractions to turn attention away from God's Word. The silent partner may need to talk to the unexpected guest who walks into the home. He should attempt to occupy disruptive children but only so much as the parents will allow. The silent partner must remain alert at all times as he watches for potential interruptions and helps to turn away any situation that would hinder his partner's presentation of the Gospel.

In conclusion, procedures will vary based on time and place, but the main objective will never change. The previous thoughts are suggestions that are proven with God's blessing. The standards and methods expressed are standards that will clearly present a "blameless" image of our Lord and Saviour. When it comes to something as important as presenting Jesus Christ to a lost world, "straddling the line" is not an option. As ambassadors for Christ, let us *"walk worthy of the vocation wherewith* [we] *are called"* (Eph. 4:1).

chapter

6

SIX

Discipleship

proper follow-up

"Then they that gladly received his word were baptized: and the same day there were added unto them about three thousand souls. And they continued stedfastly in the apostles' doctrine and fellowship, and in breaking of bread, and in prayers."—
Acts 2:41, 42.

After the soul winner leads a person to Christ, his work is only one-third completed. While the primary thought of this book deals with the salvation of lost souls, I am a strong proponent of personal follow-up and discipleship of the new believer. Granted, the salvation of the lost soul is the most important goal of soul winning, but the soul winner should not stop working with the new Christian. In fact, when a person accepts Christ, another phase of the soul winner's work begins.

*"And Jesus came and spake unto them, saying, All power is given unto me in heaven and in earth. Go ye therefore, and teach all nations, baptizing them in the name of the Father, and of the Son, and of the Holy Ghost: Teaching them to observe all things whatsoever I have commanded you: and, lo, I am with you alway, even unto the end of the world. Amen."—*Matt. 28:18–20.

Therefore, Christians have the responsibility to tell others how to be saved, to see that they are baptized, and to teach them the Word of God. These three principles are evidenced in Acts 2:41, 42: *"Then they that gladly received his word were baptized: and the same day there were added unto them about three thousand souls. And they continued stedfastly in the apostles' doctrine and fellowship, and in breaking of bread, and in prayers."*

When the people believed the teaching, they were baptized and continued steadfastly. The progression of being saved, baptized, and taught from God's Word is the natural growth process for the life of a new Christian. Any other course of growth is not natural.

The Bible teaches that a new Christian is like a newborn baby.

"As newborn babes, desire the sincere milk of the word, that ye may grow thereby" (I Pet. 2:2). In a sense, follow-up work is "spiritual pediatrics." The soul winner has the responsibility to do everything possible to help a new Christian get the right start in his Christian life. There are several steps given in the Scriptures which should be followed when working with the new Christian. Two or three of these steps may be required immediately after a person accepts Christ, depending upon the time available and an individual's desire to know more.

Assurance

The topic of assurance pertaining to salvation was covered previously, but it should be mentioned again as an area that the soul winner should discuss during his first follow-up visit to the new convert's home. First John 5:10–13 and II Timothy 1:12 teach that one can **know** that he has eternal life because Jesus Christ is powerful enough to **keep** him until the day of His return.

"He that believeth on the Son of God hath the witness in himself: he that believeth not God hath made him a liar; because he believeth not the record that God gave of his Son. And this is the record, that God hath given to us eternal life, and this life is in his Son. He that hath the Son hath life; and he that hath not the Son of God hath not life. These things have I written unto you that believe on the name of the Son of God; that ye may know that ye have eternal life, and that ye may believe on the name of the Son of God."— I John 5:10–13.

"For the which cause I also suffer these things: nevertheless I am not ashamed: for I know whom I have believed, and am persuaded that he is able to keep that which I have committed unto him against that day."— II Tim. 1:12.

Other Scriptures in the book of Ephesians also teach of the sealing power of the Holy Spirit with regard to salvation. The new convert must understand that the Lord will keep him saved and that the work for salvation is complete.

"In whom ye also trusted, after that ye heard the word of truth, the gospel

of your salvation: in whom also after that ye believed, ye were sealed with that holy Spirit of promise."—Eph.1:13.

"*And grieve not the holy Spirit of God, whereby ye are sealed unto the day of redemption.*"—Eph. 4:30.

Showing the new convert verses which tell of the surety of salvation will help solidify the decision that he has made in his heart and mind. Actually, this is more a process of reviewing the truths of salvation than it is of giving assurance. However, there are some new Christians who have the need of assurance, and they must understand the Bible's teaching on assurance and on the doctrine of eternal security. The soul winner must always be careful, however, not to give a false assurance to someone who is not saved. Only the Holy Spirit can give the assurance of salvation.

Baptism

Once a person is saved, the first act of his Christian faith is to be baptized. The Great Commission itself is a mandate that all who accept Christ are to be baptized. The New Testament has dozens of verses which teach that a believer is to be baptized.

Every soul winner knows this truth, and yet many fail to teach a new Christian the importance of being baptized. Some churches prefer to enroll a new convert in a class for several weeks and then mention baptism as a possible act of obedience. This approach is simply not scriptural—for one reason: baptism always took place immediately after salvation in the New Testament. Second, baptism is not a possible choice; it is a command to be obeyed.

The greatest disappointment of many churches is the lack of commitment on the part of new converts. Statistics have shown, if new converts are encouraged to be baptized at the next church service and to identify publicly with Christ, they show more faithfulness in the long run.

Often it is helpful for the soul winner to bring up the subject of baptism during the original soul-winning call or at the first follow-up call. It is important to share a few Scripture verses with the new

Christian to help him understand the scriptural basis for baptism. Leading the conversation into the topic will also allow you to explain that the best way to grow spiritually is to obey God's Word willfully. There are several truths related to baptism which should be taught as part of our follow-up instruction.

Baptism Identifies One With Christ

It is symbolic of one's spiritual death to the old life and his newness of life in Christ.

"Know ye not, that so many of us as were baptized into Jesus Christ were baptized into his death? Therefore we are buried with him by baptism into death: that like as Christ was raised up from the dead by the glory of the Father, even so we also should walk in newness of life."— Rom. 6:3, 4.

The Pattern of Early Christians

Christians in the early church were obedient to be baptized and were baptized soon after salvation. Baptism always followed salvation.

"Then they that gladly received his word were baptized: and the same day there were added unto them about three thousand souls."—Acts 2:41.

"But when they believed Philip preaching the things concerning the kingdom of God, and the name of Jesus Christ, they were baptized, both men and women."—Acts 8:12.

The New Christian Should Desire to Be Obedient

"And as they went on their way, they came unto a certain water: and the eunuch said, See, here is water; what doth hinder me to be baptized?"— Acts 8:36.

True Baptism Is by Immersion

"And Philip said, If thou believest with all thine heart, thou mayest. And he answered and said, I believe that Jesus Christ is the Son of God. And he

commanded the chariot to stand still: and they went down both into the water, both Philip and the eunuch; and he baptized him. And when they were come up out of the water, the Spirit of the Lord caught away Philip, that the eunuch saw him no more: and he went on his way rejoicing."— Acts 8:37–39.

Of course, there are many other Scripture verses which could be used to show to the new Christian the need for baptism. The new Christian should be carefully shown his need to be baptized and his need to become obedient to the Lord's will for his life.

Building the Confidence of the New Christian

Another reason that baptism is so important is that public profession bolsters the confidence of a new Christian. A wedding ring is a great baptism illustration. A wedding ring proudly displays that a person is married to his spouse. Without the ring, he would still be married; however, the ring publicly shows others that he is married. Baptism tells others publicly that a person has accepted Christ as his personal Saviour. If a believer is not baptized, he will still go to Heaven, as in the case of the thief on the cross; but he will not be identifying publicly with the Lord Jesus Christ.

Baptism Is Important to Christ

Public profession is important to Jesus. Matthew 10:32 says, *"Whosoever therefore shall confess me before men, him will I confess also before my Father which is in heaven."* This verse and others teach us that public profession is an important first step in the life of a new Christian. Most pastors agree that a person who will not be baptized often will not live for the Lord. The desire of a soul winner should be to help a new convert get the right start in order to lay the foundation for a healthy Christian life.

How to Be Baptized

After showing the new convert the scriptural basis for baptism, the soul winner should share practical information on the typical church procedures for baptism.

When presenting himself for baptism, the new convert should walk forward during the invitation. This would be difficult to do in many "progressive" churches which no longer have invitations. Thank God for preachers who still care enough to give invitations!

Next, a couple of counselors will take the new convert to a changing room, complete with baptismal apparel, towels and hair dryers. After the new Christian changes, the counselors will let him know when to walk down into the baptistry. The counselors should also give some instruction to the new convert about how the baptism is done. This would include what to expect the pastor to say and how the new Christian should hold his hands.

Public profession bolsters the confidence of a new Christian.

In the baptistry, the pastor will ask the new Christian if he is saved. The new Christian will say "yes," and the pastor will baptize him. After the baptism, there should be towels available, and then the counselors should help the new Christian back to the auditorium. The counselors should also take this opportunity after the baptism to have a word of prayer with the convert, giving thanks to the Lord for this special moment.

The soul winner also may want to offer to sit with the new Christian and then to walk forward with him at invitation time for his baptism. It is the soul winner's job to be a positive encouragement to the new Christian in every way possible.

Church Attendance

According to the Great Commission, after a person is saved and baptized, he is to be taught to observe the commandments of Christ. The commandments of Christ are embodied in the Bible, for Christ not only spoke personally while on this earth, but He also spoke through the human writers of God's Word by the process of inspiration.

The institution which has been established by Christ for the purpose of building up the saints is the church. God has established the local church for the purpose of giving Christians a place to assemble.

Therefore, during his follow-up, a new Christian must be instructed not to neglect the assembling together at church. Hebrews 10:25 states, *"Not forsaking the assembling of ourselves together, as the manner of some is; but exhorting one another: and so much the more, as ye see the day approaching."*

Sustaining Long-Term Faithfulness

A new convert should begin attending church right away. Personal follow-up efforts should not go on indefinitely. Soon the personal follow-up will become minimal in order to give way to the corporate follow-up of the church. This schedule includes pastoral visits, Sunday school visits, and possibly other personal Bible study options as provided by the church. Thus, the only long-term and vital teaching that the new Christian must learn to depend upon is the teaching of his pastor, his Sunday school teacher and his own Bible study. This is the progression from the need for consistent follow-up, as a newborn babe, to the ability which comes with maturity to feed oneself and to receive feeding for oneself at church. Of course the friendship of the new Christian and the soul winner will go on until the Lord returns, but there are many opportunities of growth in the church program besides the few personal times with the soul winner.

Although the new Christian should begin attending church immediately after salvation, he may not be desirous of faithful church attendance until the follow-up process has been completed. The exact number of weeks that the soul winner should continue to visit the home of a new Christian for follow-up depends upon the individual. Normally two to four visits are plenty if the time is used wisely. The soul winner must be cautious that the new

Follow-up must not become home Bible study that takes the place of attending church.

Christian's follow-up does not become a home Bible study that takes the place of attending church.

Although his intentions may be innocent, a soul winner can actually divert a new Christian away from church by offering him extensive follow-up. It is the pastor's responsibility to *equip the saints for the work of the ministry.* As the soul winner performs his work, he is wise to channel a new Christian to church, where he too may become equipped for the work of the ministry.

One must remember that God has ordained the foolishness of preaching to confound the wise. No soul winner should choose to get a new Christian off to a slow start by having him attend a home Bible study rather than having him be a part of God's ordained institution, the church. Of course I am talking primarily of a Biblically correct, noncompromising church.

Ingredients of a Good Church

Each Christian needs to be involved in a local church where he cannot only be taught, but where he can serve and grow. The church can be likened to a planter box of fertile soil where a new Christian is placed for spiritual growth. There are several ingredients which are present in the "planter box" of a good church: the fertile soil of fellowship, the nutrients for growth provided by the preaching and the teaching, water from the Word of God, the sunshine of opportunity for Christian service, and protection from the weeds of false doctrine. A pastor who does his gardening will weed out false doctrine.

It has been observed that a new Christian who is planted in the "planter box" of a local church has a greater chance for Christian growth than the new Christian who neglects church attendance. Each soul winner should remember that the word *church* or *ecclesia* is mentioned 117 times in the New Testament, and over 100 of these instances refer to the local assemblies of saved, baptized believers. Each of these assemblies had a pastor and deacons, and they met regularly to preach and to teach the teachings of Christ. These churches also had doctrinal positions which separated them from false teachers.

> A Christian who is planted in the "planter box" of a local church has a greater chance for Christian growth.

Many people today are not willing to become involved in God's institution, the local church. In some cases, they reject church attendance because they do not want to be baptized, do not agree with the pastor, or are unwilling to submit themselves to spiritual authority as mentioned in Hebrews 13:17: *"Obey them that have the rule over you, and submit yourselves: for they watch for your souls, as they that must give account, that they may do it with joy, and not with grief: for that is unprofitable for you."*

During the follow-up with the new Christian, the soul winner must stress the importance of meeting regularly at church for spiritual growth in obedience to the Lord. The new Christian needs to realize that there is no good reason for refusing to attend a good, Bible-believing church.

Follow-up work is in fact "spiritual pediatrics." Soul winners must do their part to help the babes in Christ remain healthy during the early days of their Christian lives.

Personal Devotions

As the soul winner works with a new convert, his goal is to see that the new Christian becomes established in the Faith. Paul wrote in Colossians 2:6–8, *"As ye have therefore received Christ Jesus the Lord, so walk ye in him: Rooted and built up in him, and stablished in the faith, as ye have been taught, abounding therein with thanksgiving. Beware lest any man spoil you through philosophy and vain deceit, after the tradition of men, after the rudiments of the world, and not after Christ."*

These verses summarize the desired goals in the life of every

Christian, and the application is especially important to a babe in Christ. The verses show the progression in the new Christian's life. First, he receives Christ; then he begins to walk in Christ, to be rooted in Him and to be grounded in Him. The new Christian then becomes established in the Faith through the teaching of the man of God for whom he is thankful. He develops discernment so as not to fall prey to the philosophies of men and continues diligently in the truth of God's Word.

The thought of seeing a new Christian grow and mature in the Lord is indeed very exciting. It is a wonderful thing to see a person follow these steps of Christian growth and maturity which are found in Colossians 2:6–8. The resounding question of many ardent soul winners is: "How can we see this goal of Christian maturity accomplished?"

The key is found in the vital area of follow-up. The soul winner must give the new convert direction in the Christian's walk with Christ in order that the new Christian may become established in the Faith. Not only must a soul winner encourage the new convert to be baptized but also to attend church.

Yet beyond these local church related aspects of growth, the two greatest areas for which a new Christian needs direction are *prayer* and *Bible study*. Once again, the need is not so much for the soul winner to spend session after session in prayer and teaching the Bible but rather for the soul winner to teach the new Christian the *importance* of prayer and how to study the Bible.

The soul winner will definitely want to teach some spiritual truths during the first few follow-up calls, but the goal is to teach the new Christian how to read the Bible and how to pray on his own. The new Christian will naturally depend upon solid Bible teaching and preaching for growth, but he must also be encouraged to spend time personally with the Lord every day.

To help a new Christian begin a personal time with the Lord each day, the soul winner should encourage him to set aside a specific time each day for systematic Bible study. He may recommend a book of the Bible in which to begin, perhaps John or

The goal is to see that the new Christian becomes established in the Faith.

Philippians. The new Christian should be encouraged to write down observations from what he reads in God's Word, to apply the Scripture personally, and to seek what possible changes are needed in his own life and write these thoughts down. On follow-up visits, the soul winner should always ask the new Christian if he has had the opportunity to study the Scriptures and if he has any questions or comments to share.

The soul winner also needs to suggest that the new Christian spend time in prayer before and after his Bible reading. He should tell the new Christian that before Bible reading, he needs to ask the Holy Spirit to guide him into all truth (John 16:13). After Bible reading, the new Christian needs to ask God's help in applying the Biblical principles to his life. He may also pray for needs in his life, such as unsaved loved ones, finances, spiritual growth, employment, etc. He may want to keep a list of things for which he is praying and mark the list when a prayer is answered.

These are very basic guidelines for prayer and for Bible study. A new Christian must be encouraged to begin a new life in Christ by drawing close to Him through personal daily devotions.

The reason for encouraging the new Christian to have personal devotional time is to encourage obedience to Christ in these basic areas so that he may grow in the Lord. There are several verses which teach the importance of personal devotions in the Word of God each day. These verses are helpful to share with a new convert on the second follow-up visit.

Bible Study in Personal Devotions

"All scripture is given by inspiration of God, and is profitable for doctrine, for reproof, for correction, for instruction in righteousness: That the man of God may be perfect, throughly furnished unto all good works."—II Tim. 3:16, 17.

"Let the word of Christ dwell in you richly in all wisdom; teaching and admonishing one another in psalms and hymns and spiritual songs, singing with grace in your hearts to the Lord."—Col. 3:16.

"Take heed unto thyself, and unto the doctrine; continue in them: for in doing this thou shalt both save thyself, and them that hear thee."—I Tim. 4:16.

"Study to shew thyself approved unto God, a workman that needeth not to be ashamed, rightly dividing the word of truth."—II Tim. 2:15.

"For the word of God is quick, and powerful, and sharper than any twoedged sword, piercing even to the dividing asunder of soul and spirit, and of the joints and marrow, and is a discerner of the thoughts and intents of the heart."—Heb. 4:12.

Prayer in Personal Devotions

"Let us therefore come boldly unto the throne of grace, that we may obtain mercy, and find grace to help in time of need."—Heb. 4:16.

"And he spake a parable unto them to this end, that men ought always to pray, and not to faint."—Luke 18:1.

"Pray without ceasing."—I Thess. 5:17.

"Be careful for nothing; but in every thing by prayer and supplication with thanksgiving let your requests be made known unto God. And the peace of God, which passeth all understanding, shall keep your hearts and minds through Christ Jesus."—Phil. 4:6,7.

"I exhort therefore, that, first of all, supplications, prayers, intercessions, and giving of thanks, be made for all men."—I Tim. 2:1.

"Watch and pray, that ye enter not into temptation: the spirit indeed is willing, but the flesh is weak."—Matt. 26:41.

In our church in Lancaster, California, we have an extensive personal discipleship course for every new Christian, which is made possible through an adult Bible class and in conjunction with our midweek Bible study. Through this program our new converts are personally matched with a trained discipler for thirteen weeks of personal training and faith building. The initial follow-up pointers found in this book are intended to bridge the gap from the time a person is saved until he is enrolled in a systematic study of God's Word.

The Importance of Fellowship

Another vital ingredient in the growth of the new Christian which must be stressed during the follow-up process is fellowship. Christian fellowship is a real need in the life of a new Christian; however, Christian fellowship must be kept in proper balance. Many churches provide many activities for the purpose of fellowship, yet neglect the teaching and the preaching of God's Word.

As seen in Acts, chapter 2, and in other New Testament passages, fellowship is an integral part of a growing church. It is important that the new Christian develop spiritual relationships with godly people who will be an encouragement to him. It is a blessing for the new convert to experience fellowship as a new member of God's family with his brothers and sisters in Christ.

The joy of Christian fellowship will be experienced by a new Christian if the soul winner initiates fellowship by inviting the new Christian to an evening in his home or to a church activity.

Personal Responsibility Is the Key

A soul winner should have a personal sense of responsibility for the new Christian in the area of fellowship. When an individual accepts Christ, a soul winner should be very happy but should not be completely satisfied. He should continue to fellowship with the new Christian until that person is grounded in the Faith.

A person may wonder what this emphasis on fellowship has to do with grounding someone in the Faith. When discussing the importance of fellowship with a new convert, the *replacement concept* should be explained. Since this person has passed from death unto life and has been commanded to walk as a child of light, there are certain areas of his life that may need to be given up completely. The idea of giving up the old social life and old habits can be very frightening to a new Christian unless he learns the truth that *God will never ask him to give up something without replacing it with something better.* God wants us to replace the old life with a new life in Christ.

Fellowship is an important part of the *replacement concept* because many newly saved men and women will need to replace the bar crowd or the social crowd at work with church activities and Christian friends.

A Christian who wants salvation but who neither wants to give up his old social life nor wants to fellowship at God's house or with God's people, cannot expect God's blessing. To experience these blessings, a new Christian must fellowship with his brothers and sisters in Christ; therefore, his brothers and sisters in Christ should offer him opportunities for developing Christian friendships.

Fellowship With a Purpose

A Christian should always remember to fellowship with a purpose. The purpose of Christian fellowship is to glorify Christ and to draw others closer to Him. This goal should be remembered when involving new Christians. There are several guidelines that are helpful to follow:

- Speak about things which will be useful for the spiritual edification of the new Christian.

- Speak highly of the church and of the pastoral staff.

- Talk about the joys of being a Christian.

- Introduce the new Christian to other Christians.

- Have patience with the new Christian who has not yet learned to control his vocabulary and habits.

- Have the home in spotless condition.

- Do not attempt to act as the pastor and have a mini church service.

- Do not fellowship with the same people repeatedly.

- End the fellowship in prayer to God thanking Him for fellowship through Christ.

The Importance of Soul Winning

I believe a new Christian should also be challenged to share his faith with others soon after his salvation. In the Great Commission, Matthew 28:20, Jesus says, *"Teaching them to observe all things whatsoever I have commanded you: and, lo, I am with you alway, even unto the end of the world."* As Jesus gave His instructions for follow-up, He commanded that His commandments be taught.

Apart from verse 20, His final commandments are found in verse 19, which states, *"Go ye therefore, and teach all nations, baptizing them in the name of the Father, and of the Son, and of the Holy Ghost."*

Since we are to teach His commandments to the new Christian, we should definitely teach him the great and final commandment, to lead lost souls to Jesus Christ.

While at times it may seem to make more sense to cushion the new Christian by not encouraging him to become actively involved in Christian service until a year or so after salvation, generally, the contrary is true. The people whom I have seen become soul winners right away after salvation are the same ones who have grown stronger and faster in the Lord. This is because they have been obedient to the Lord by fulfilling His Great Commission.

Also, a new Christian will grow in spiritual knowledge as he is confronted with the challenges and questions that arise in active soul winning. These new Christians will increase in boldness for the Lord and will grow in their dependence upon Him.

> Those who become soul winners right away after salvation grow stronger and faster in the Lord.

It should be stated, however, that churches must be very careful about giving too much responsibility to the new Christian too soon. However, this principle of teaching the new Christian to be a soul winner is essential and is found in II Timothy 2:2: *"And the things that thou hast heard of me among many witnesses, the same commit thou to faithful men, who shall be able to teach others also."*

While Timothy would not be classified as a new Christian, Paul does instruct Timothy to seek out others who can be taught the truth. In turn, these faithful men were to win and to train others for the Lord. When Paul said, *"And the things that thou hast heard of me...,"* there was an obvious reference not only to the broader scope of Paul's teaching, but also to the specific teaching of salvation. Paul's commandment to Timothy was to keep busy winning souls and training the new Christians to win souls as well. This method of committing the Gospel to men and training them to tell others is God's plan for reaching the world.

Nothing Replaces Personal Soul Winning

In the past few decades there has been a great emphasis on television ministries and citywide crusades. While both of these approaches can be helpful, there is no substitute for God's plan of personal soul winning and follow-up. The need today is not for the businessman in church simply to give money for a TV ministry. The need today is for the businessman to give financially *and to be a soul winner* at work and through his church ministry. The need today is not only for preachers to hold citywide meetings, but also to hold person-to-person soul-winning appointments until the Lord returns. Since soul winning is God's plan for reaching the world, then new converts must be trained to be the faithful men that Paul speaks about in II Timothy 2 and be encouraged to teach others also.

Being an Example

The final step in the area of follow-up does not require effort on the part of the new Christian. This step revolves entirely around the soul winner and his responsibility to be an example to the new Christian. Every soul winner should be conscious of the fact that he is being observed by the new convert and consequently should endeavor to be a godly example before him or her.

One evening several years ago, I was at home reading a book, and my daughter, who was then four years old, sat down next to me and began "reading" a book. A few minutes later, I noticed that she was holding her book the same way I was holding mine, and her legs were crossed in the same manner as mine were crossed. Whenever I would turn a page, she would turn a page. Every action I made was copied by her.

All parents can relate to the way children sometimes repeat their actions, regardless of whether the actions are good or bad. Those with children are very careful to set the proper example for them.

There is an obvious parallel in the relationship between parents and their children, and that of the soul winner and his spiritual children. Every new Christian will naturally watch and often copy the actions of the person who led him to Christ. This puts a great amount of responsibility on the soul winner to be the right example.

Obviously, the goal is to direct others to follow the example of Jesus Christ and of Him alone. After all, any soul winner will eventually fail the new Christian if the new Christian watches him closely enough. Yet the fact remains that every Christian has been influenced and directed by various spiritual leaders during his Christian life.

To understand further the importance of setting a proper example, one may observe the Apostle Paul's relationship to the Christians at Thessalonica.

"For our gospel came not unto you in word only, but also in power, and in the Holy Ghost, and in much assurance; as ye know what manner of men we were among you for your sake. And ye became followers of us, and of the Lord, having received the word in much affliction, with joy of the Holy Ghost: So that ye were ensamples to all that believe in Macedonia and Achaia."—I Thess. 1:5–7.

There are three important steps to notice from these verses in regard to setting an example for the new Christian.

Step One: Paul was the right example (verse 5). *"...ye know what manner of men we were among you for your sake."*

Step Two: The Thessalonians followed Paul's example (verse 6). *"And ye became followers of us, and of the Lord."*

Step Three: The Thessalonians became examples (verse 7). *"So that ye were ensamples."*

The progression of spiritual growth as mentioned in these three verses is exactly what godly soul winners should desire to see accomplished. It should be their goal that, because of their faithful presentation of the Gospel and their faithful example, God will work in the hearts of those to whom they witness and will bring to completion His will for their lives.

The matter of follow-up and discipleship may not always seem glamorous, but it is the vital link that must be provided from birth to maturity. Let me encourage you now to stick with the new Christian and love him to spiritual maturity.

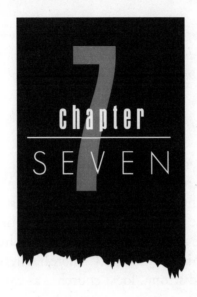

chapter

SEVEN

7

Priorities

of the church

"Now therefore ye are no more strangers and foreigners,
but fellowcitizens with the saints, and of the
household of God."—Eph. 2:19.

We have already stressed in this book the importance of the local church as it relates to the carrying out of the Great Commission, as well as the establishing of new Christians in basic Bible truth. Indeed, the church is the pillar and ground of truth (I Tim. 3:15, 16). It is the responsibility of each local church to uphold the truth of God within a community. There has never been a day when our world needed strong, local churches as we do in this hour of world history!

A Clearly Defined Strategy

A local church that has a clearly defined strategy of ministry will be a tremendous blessing not only to the soul winner but also to the new Christians. Ephesians 4 tells us that it is the responsibility of pastors to equip the saints "for the work of the ministry." Each pastor of a local church must dedicate himself to developing a program that is user-friendly for the dedicated soul winners in the local church. This would include not only the establishment of programs within the church but also the establishment of clearly defined lines of communication and the provision of quality materials and training for the soul winner.

Indeed, the pastor and leadership of a church that is conscientious about reaching and training people for the Lord Jesus Christ, must be continually developing their ministry philosophy according to the foundational truths of God's Word and the ever expanding needs of their own local church.

Committed to Personal Growth

This requires the personal growth of the pastor, as well as the organizational growth of the church. The Apostle Paul stated in Philippians 3:13, *"Brethren, I count not myself to have apprehended."* Truly, any pastor who is desiring to be used of God realizes the importance of continually growing on a personal level in order to meet the needs of a church family as a whole.

Vision will not be sustained in a church unless there is a properly defined strategy of ministry.

As a pastor grows in the Word of God and in his faith concerning the Christian life, inevitably God will give him some form of spiritual vision for the work to which He has called him. As the pastor communicates this vision to the congregation, oftentimes there is a great amount of excitement and determination to accomplish something great for God. Most pastors and church leaders, at some point in time, have experienced the joy of sharing their vision and having others join them in the excitement to accomplish something great for God. However, vision and excitement will not be sustained in the context of the soul winner's life nor in the context of the local church unless there are properly defined direction and strategy of ministry provided in the local church.

As a pastor, I am constantly challenging the members of our church to be involved in soul winning and outreach; however, I also have determined to do my best with regard to the development of a ministry program that encourages and edifies our church family, while providing various opportunities for the new Christian to become involved in the church family and grow in the grace and knowledge of our Lord Jesus Christ.

Establishing and Refining Clear Priorities

A part of this leadership process has been to establish clearly defined priorities of our church program and then to show our church members how each ministry directly supports one of the priorities of the church. Although these concepts have been present since the beginning of our ministry, we have continually worked to refine them and make them more understandable and workable as the years have passed.

Inspire a Heart for God

Our first priority, as a church, is to glorify Christ in His church by inspiring people to develop a heart for God. As hearts are lifted in worship to Christ during every service, He is glorified and pleased. Every week there are people who attend the church services who have either never accepted Christ as Saviour or who have made a previous decision but have since grown spiritually cold. Therefore, it is our stated purpose that each service would help people develop a greater heart for God. By this we mean either through accepting Christ as Saviour or through a decision of commitment and dedication to the Lord.

Ministries That Inspire

We accomplish this priority primarily through the preaching and music ministries of the church. It is our hope that through a carefully planned music ministry and prayerfully prepared preaching, God will work in the hearts of those we have invited to attend our services. Nothing is more discouraging for a soul winner than when he invites a friend to church and the service is ill prepared and not at all inspiring with respect to spiritual growth and motivation. The psalmist says in Psalm 34:1–3, *"I will bless the LORD at all times: his praise shall continually be in my mouth. My soul shall make her boast in the LORD: the humble shall hear thereof, and be glad. O magnify the LORD with me, and let us exalt his name together."* The goal of our service is to magnify the name of the Lord through proper worship.

Our worship style includes very conservative, godly music in accordance with Ephesians 5:19, which states, *"Speaking to yourselves in psalms and hymns and spiritual songs, singing and making melody in your heart to the Lord."* These are songs of praise unto the

Lord. Our singing, whether of hymns or choruses, should always be from our hearts unto the Lord and should also be a testimony to those who are visiting with us concerning our love for Christ. Music in which the melody is predominant and whose lyrics are doctrinally sound, will glorify Christ. This is God-honoring music. It has been our experience that when visitors hear music that is distinct from that of the world, oftentimes their hearts are touched in an unusually powerful way.

The Place of Preaching

The primary focus of true Biblical worship, however, is the preaching of the Word of God. In today's Christian culture, most people associate the term *worship* with some type of a praise band approach. But New Testament worship always focused on the preaching of the Word of God. Second Timothy 4:2 states, *"Preach the word; be instant in season, out of season; reprove, rebuke, exhort with all longsuffering and doctrine."*

America is dying because of a lack of strong, Bible-based preaching. Nothing will inspire a person to come to God any more than old-fashioned, Bible-based preaching of the Word of God. If we are truly desiring to inspire people to develop a heart for God, we must endeavor to rightly divide the Word of Truth in their midst in order that their response, whatever it may be, will be based upon the Word of God.

> The primary focus of true Biblical worship is the preaching of the Word of God.

Of course, the primary objective in our preaching ought to be to lift up the name of the Lord Jesus Christ, to exalt and magnify Him as our Saviour and Lord.

Supporting the Pillar of Preaching

With this purpose in mind, we also have several ministries working together to inspire people to develop a heart for God. The first and foremost would be the pulpit ministry. The pastors and teachers of our church prayerfully prepare each message, asking God to lift people closer to Himself through the messages. Other ministries which support this purpose are the choir and orchestra ministries. The choir and orchestra members pray and prepare diligently, asking God to use them in preparing the hearts of men and women for preaching.

Also, those involved in the sound and maintenance ministries play an important part in preparing the physical aspect of the service and buildings. Cleanliness in a building will help people worship, and a lack of cleanliness will distract and even hinder worship. If those involved in the maintenance of a building will realize they are doing something which will inspire worship, it will place an entirely new perspective on their service rendered unto the Lord Jesus Christ.

As we endeavor to impact our area for Christ, we are making contacts with thousands of people over the course of a year's time. However, the matter of inspiring them through Biblical worship will not take place until the new Christian or the person who is yet considering his need for Christ, attends the services of your church.

Include People in the Church Family

Once an individual has accepted Christ as Saviour, either at church or through the organized soul-winning program of the church, it should be our desire to include him as a part of the church family. Acts 2:41 states, *"Then they that gladly received his word were baptized: and the same day there were added unto them about three thousand souls."* The believers at the early New Testament churches were added to a particular number of believers and began to fellowship within that context. People need a family or a place where they are loved and where they belong. Ephesians 2:19 says, *"Now therefore ye are no more strangers and foreigners, but fellowcitizens with the saints, and of the household of God."* God says one is not a stranger or foreigner spiritually once he becomes a part of the family of God.

Being included in a church family takes place in different ways for different situations. For example, if a person begins to visit an adult Bible class, he will be included through the process of enrollment into that class, although he is not yet a member of the church. Whatever the situation, we want every visitor to feel included and welcome as soon as he arrives on the church property.

Included Through Membership

Specifically, however, we believe the Bible teaches that every person should be included as an identifiable member of a local assembly. Membership is accomplished in two basic ways: First, the person who has accepted Christ through the soul-winning outreach of the church may follow the Lord in believer's baptism and become a member through baptism. Second, someone who has accepted Christ and has been baptized previously in a church of like faith may become a member through his statement of faith in Christ.

On a practical level, those involved in the baptism ministry are also helping people to be included by preparing the baptistry apparel, towels, etc. Although, again, this would be a support type of ministry, it is certainly a vital ministry in the process of helping people as they identify with Christ and the local church.

Included Through Fellowship

Once a person has been included as a member of the church, there are many opportunities of fellowship and service which he or she will enjoy on a more personal and intimate level.

Ministries that support the purpose of including people in the church would be as follows:

The soul-winning ministry—As the soul winner carries out his follow-up visits, he will encourage people to be baptized and to be included in the church family.

The Sunday school ministry—The Sunday school teachers are also working to encourage the people who have attended their classes to become a part of the church family as well.

Care groups—Each adult class has small groups of people who are responsible to welcome and care for a small handful of class members. Through these groups and their related fellowship times, new attendees feel at home with friends who really love them.

Ministry activities—Every activity for every age group is carried out with a purpose in mind. Part of the purpose of these fun times is to include people in the family.

The ways to include a person in the love and care of your church family are as endless as your creativity. The initial goal is to communicate a loving spirit of acceptance. The ultimate goal is to lead a Christian to commit himself to membership in your church where he considers himself a part of the family. When a person is included in your church, it is no longer just "your church" or "that church"—it is to him "my church!"

Instruct People From God's Word

Instructed Through Preaching and Teaching

Once a person has been included as a member of a local church, our primary mandate from Scripture is to instruct him from the Word of God. Acts 2:42: *"And they continued stedfastly in the apostles' doctrine and fellowship, and in breaking of bread, and in prayers."* Therefore, we encourage every new Christian and new member to attend the regular preaching services of the church and to enroll in an adult Bible class. There he will be instructed in God's Word through the teaching and preaching of pastors and teachers who have prepared Bible lessons. Dr. Lee Roberson of Chattanooga, Tennessee, coined the phrase "Three to Thrive." It is his conviction that the Sunday morning, Sunday night, and Wednesday night services should be carried out on a grand level. Following his counsel, we have a choir sing at each of these services, and we encourage all of our members to

> The pulpit ministry and the adult Bible class ministry work together to edify people.

attend these times of assembly for the local church.

Furthermore, our adult Bible class teachers are trained in teaching the Word of God. In our local church, we believe that leaders should lead, teachers should teach, and helpers should help. It is vital that those who are involved in a teaching ministry have the gift of teaching and the desire to serve the Lord in this capacity. The adult class should truly be a place of instruction. Although there will be fellowship and other opportunities for Christian growth, the primary purpose is the instruction of the Word of God.

Thus, the pulpit ministry and the adult Bible class ministry are working together to edify people, or to build them up in their faith. Our objective in this respect is to bring the new Christians to maturity. It is important that we stress the fact that maturity involves more than the acquisition of knowledge, but the application of that knowledge as well. Therefore, each message or lesson is concluded with a challenge or an application. *"But be ye doers of the word, and not hearers only, deceiving your own selves"* (Jas. 1:22).

Instructed Through Personal Discipleship

Within each adult Bible class, there is also a unique opportunity in our local church for the one-on-one training of a new believer. Each adult class has men and women who are trained in personally discipling a new believer one-on-one. Basically, when a person is baptized or added to the church, he is contacted by the discipleship secretary of the church and asked if he would like to have this type of training. We have already previously mentioned that the soul winner will make a few follow-up visits, and he will always maintain a contact with the person that was saved; however, the bulk of the follow-up and discipleship will be transferred to the particular adult Bible class where the person is enrolled.

> Believers need the opportunity to ask questions as their lives are developing spiritually.

Consequently, the church offers not only the opportunity for corporate gathering and growth, but it also offers the opportunity for individual grounding in the Word of God. The discipleship ministry, which operates through the adult Bible classes, affords a new believer the opportunity to ask questions as his life is developing spiritually.

Over the years pastors and church leaders will be asked to define their ministries. Sometimes someone may ask, "Do you have a soul-winning church?" The answer should be "yes!" On other occasions we are asked, "Do you have a church that believes in worship?" The answer should be "yes." Every church should provide services that inspire people to develop a heart for God. Then there are those who may ask, "Does your church make people feel welcome and offer opportunities for fellowship?" Again, the answer is "yes," and we have ministries to support the purpose of including people in the church family. Then, many times people will ask, "Does your church instruct and teach people from the Word of God?" Again, the answer is "yes." All of these purposes are designed to comple-ment the soul-winning ministry of the church and encourage the individual soul winner. Not only will the soul winner of the local church benefit from the well-structured and clearly defined pur-pose of the church, but the new Christian will also begin to benefit as well.

Involving People in the Ministry of Christ

Once the new Christian has grown through the preaching and teaching of God's Word in the context of the local church, our goal is to involve that person in the ministry himself. *"As every man hath received the gift, even so minister the same one to another, as good stewards of the manifold grace of God"* (I Pet. 4:10).

When a person accepts Christ as Saviour, he receives divine enabling through the Holy Spirit of God and spiritual gifts whereby he may serve the Lord Jesus Christ. Over the course of time, as he is instructed in the Word of God, a new believer will begin to learn of ways and areas where he may serve the Lord more effectively. A new Christian may desire, for example, to help, teach or serve, as he understands his God-given gifts and as he grows in an under-standing of the Word of God.

It has been said, "Tell me, and I will forget. Show me, and I will remember. Involve me, and I will understand." It is our goal to involve everyone in ministry in order that he might more completely understand the Word of God.

Each Person Has a Place in the Body

It is at this point that the ministry comes full circle. Now we are seeing those who have been saved becoming involved in serving the Lord Jesus Christ themselves. What an exciting time this is for the original soul winner as well as the new Christian!

God has graciously given each of us the ability to serve Him. He has gifted us with spiritual gifts and empowered us by His grace. We, then, must find our place in the body of Christ and be faithful to serve the Lord Jesus Christ. Two of the most often quoted phrases in our ministry have been "Every saint is a servant" and "Every member is a minister."

We must not ever view the staff as our "paid soul winners." We must view the pastoral staff of the church as those who equip others for the work of the ministry. While I personally believe that every pastor should be a soul winner, I believe that his task must also include training others to be soul winners. Consequently, all the saints will be serving and ministering together and accomplishing more for the glory of God.

Protecting Doctrinal Purity While Maintaining Cultural Sensitivity

Two points should be quickly understood with respect to the philosophy of ministry as we approach the twenty-first century. First, every pastor and every Christian leader should be very careful, in these days, to maintain a doctrinal distinctiveness and direction within the ministry. Everyone involved in ministry must be committed to the doctrinal statement of the church and should be able to defend that position clearly and Biblically.

Second, the church leadership must strive to be sensitive to the growing and expanding needs of our culture. By making this statement, we are not implying that a church should capitulate to pragmatism in regard to ministry approach and philosophy. We will never inspire people to develop a heart for God if we are using a fleshly or carnal approach to the ministry.

However, I believe it is possible to be doctrinally sound and remain sensitive to the culture of our community. For example, in our community there are thousands of Spanish-speaking people. As we have attempted to be aware of this need, it has been a joy to establish a growing Spanish ministry, which is meeting the needs of hundreds of people each week.

> It is possible to be doctrinally sound and remain sensitive to the culture of our communities.

We must prayerfully see the needs and then, by God's grace, endeavor to meet the needs within our community. We must also train those who are involved in ministry to be sensitive to the ever-changing culture. This sensitivity must not be gained for the purpose of changing our message but for the purpose of relating it in understandable terms whereby men and women may still be saved and involved in the local church ministry.

I do not believe that churches today need to abandon terms such as *atonement* or *justification;* however, I do believe we need to take the time to define these terms to those who perhaps have never been exposed to the Word of God. This does not involve the changing of doctrine. It merely involves maintaining a sensitive heart, first, toward the Word of God and, second, toward the needs of lost men and women everywhere.

Equipping the Saints for the Ministry

It is vital that a person who has been saved any length of time become involved in ministry, but it is equally vital that we continue equipping him once he is involved in ministry. This takes place through various training seminars and the ongoing, in-house training of the local church.

It is vital that we purposefully equip Christians to serve Christ in ministry.

One real tragedy in many churches is simply that people are placed into ministry without any proving, training, or equipping process. Oftentimes I have heard people tell me they have been made trustees or youth workers at a church after having attended for only a few months. We must be careful to allow time for a person to become grounded and for his testimony to be established before he is thrust into ministry.

Again, once he is involved in ministry, continuing education is a key for the future of the person involved, as well as the ministry in which he serves. We must realize that we are dealing with something much more valuable than a multimillion-dollar jet. We are dealing with the precious souls of men, and it is important that we do not involve someone in ministry who has not first been proven. *"Lay hands suddenly on no man"* (I Tim. 5:22).

Impacting Your Region and Your World With the Gospel

At the beginning of our ministry we realized that our desire was to impact our area with the Gospel of Jesus Christ. Acts 1:8 says, *"But ye shall receive power, after that the Holy Ghost is come upon you: and ye shall be witnesses unto me both in Jerusalem, and in all Judæa, and in Samaria, and unto the uttermost part of the earth."* This is the commission of the church. We are to go out and impact regions of our world for the Lord Jesus Christ. In the general sense, every church member needs to realize that he is an ambassador for the Lord Jesus Christ. Also, in the context of Acts 1:8, we need to teach Christians today that we are to be involved in soul winning and evangelism not only in our local area but also by supporting missionaries around the world. It has been our goal to add ten to twelve missionaries each year to our missions budget as we endeavor to follow the commission of Acts 1:8.

Saturation Evangelism

When we speak to our people about the purpose of impacting our area for Christ, we are, of course, speaking of evangelism. It is our desire that no one would move into our community and live there for any length of time without hearing about the Gospel of Jesus Christ and without receiving an invitation to church. One primary way we accomplish this task is through our saturation evangelism. This approach, which is carried out by several hundred members on a weekly basis, is where we go from door to door throughout the community inviting people to attend our church. These soul winners are trained to take every opportunity to lead people to the Lord at that first contact, and yet they are also told not to feel as though they have failed if this is merely a time of sowing the seed of the Gospel of Christ.

Every time we go from our church out into the community, we are fishing for men. Our intent is to tell people about Christ and to see them accept Him as their Saviour. Even if someone does not accept Christ during this time of soul winning, we want to bear in mind that we have still been obedient to the Lord in doing our part by going and telling others.

Training Personal Soul Winners

Although our church often uses television commercials and we have daily radio broadcasts and other forms of outreach, nothing can ever replace personally contacting people as representatives of our Lord Jesus Christ. Our stated purpose is to impact our area aggressively with the Gospel of Christ. This is done primarily through a program called TEAM Soul Winning (Train Every Available Member). The TEAM soul winners are trained

> Every church member needs to realize that he is an ambassador for the Lord Jesus Christ.

on Tuesday mornings or evenings using the material found in this book. As we go out to impact our area for Christ, there are different types of calls that are used. Some are contact calls. These are follow-up calls on people we have already met through referrals from relatives, or they are to people who have visited our church. Then, of course, there are the door-to-door visits.

The Bus Ministry

Another ministry that falls under impacting our area would be the bus ministry. I personally thank God for the bus ministry, if for no reason other than the fact that in the 1970s a bus captain knocked on the door of my wife, Terrie, and invited her to attend Sunday school. It was through his persistent and caring ministry that my wife accepted Christ as a young teenager in San Jose, California. Although many churches have given up on the concept of busing people to church, I believe, as we approach the twenty-first century, that the bus ministry is still a tremendous way to impact people's lives with the Gospel of Christ. Nearly every community has boys and girls who will never come to church unless we go and bring them in. The dedicated bus workers of our church ministry realize that they are impacting our area with the Gospel of Christ.

Special Sundays of Outreach

Also, as we endeavor to impact our area for Christ, we schedule several special days throughout the calendar year which are intended to be used by our church members as special opportunities for inviting friends to church. It may be something as simple as a Friend Day or something uniquely tailored to a community. In our case, we have used a special Sunday called "Commuter Sunday" where we honor all of those who commute more than one hour to work. We give them a special gift package and prepare a special message with their needs in mind. Of course, their primary need is the Gospel of Christ, and it has been our joy on an annual basis to see many of these commuters accept Christ.

Community-Related Events

While most of these special outreach events take place on Sunday, we also need to realize that our Easter and Christmas musicals should each be viewed as a primary time for reaching the lost with the Gospel of Christ. Special events such as these are often the first time that someone will visit a church and a great time for planting the seed of the Gospel. In our case, it is a great time to give a brief gospel message and invite people to trust Christ as Saviour.

While impacting an area for Christ is a relatively basic concept in the Christian life, it must be a priority for the church. Again we are reminded that Jesus came to seek and to save the lost.

Five Priorities Working Together

These are the Biblical priorities of the church—to inspire, to include, to instruct, to involve, and to impact—and they are the priorities that we have chosen to make an integral part of Lancaster Baptist Church. The important truth to remember is that each of these priorities must be upheld and carried out in conjunction with the other four. All five of these priorities are carried out at once as the church family grows in God's grace. Every ministry of the church should fulfill one of these priorities, and every priority should have ministries that support and fulfill it. If this is not the case, then they are not really *priorities*.

Understanding, teaching and carrying out these priorities give the leadership and the church family a sense of common purpose and vision. They define direction and unite hearts behind a Biblical cause. Failing to define and communicate priorities such as these weakens the team effort of the church to glorify Christ and fulfill His plan.

chapter

EIGHT

Organizing

a soul-winning ministry

"Let all things be done decently and in order."—
I Cor.14:40.

I am convinced that most Christians at some point in their Christian walk have a strong desire to be involved in reaching others for Christ. I am equally convinced that God has ordained pastors and teachers for the purpose of equipping the saints "for the work of the ministry." Because of this conviction, we write this chapter to help pastors, teachers and soul winners work together in establishing a local church soul-winning ministry.

When the Apostle Paul wrote to Timothy with regard to the work of the ministry, he admonished him to commit the truth to faithful men who would "teach others also" (II Tim. 2:2).

The Word of God further reminds us that the church is "the pillar and ground of the truth" (I Tim. 3:15).

Every pastor and church member must understand that God has called individuals to share the Gospel, and the primary institution in which God's people are to be trained and from which they are to be sent is the local church.

One of the reasons more Christians are not actively involved in reaching the lost is that churches are not strategically planning to win souls and disciple them in the Faith.

In this chapter we will look at the philosophy of the local church soul-winning program as well as some practical consider-ations for establishing an outreach program in a local church.

The Purpose of the Soul-Winning Ministry

It may seem basic, but there is a need to stop and ask, "Why start a soul-winning program?" This program should not be established merely for the sake of adding a program. Most churches today have calendars full of activities and meetings. The soul-winning program should not be established merely to add numbers to the church. The Bible teaches that the Lord adds to the church. Jesus is building His church today! The only right purpose for establishing a local church soul-winning program is a conviction based upon Scriptures that we must as a church endeavor to reach our own "Jerusalem" with the Gospel of Jesus Christ.

The following purposes will be fulfilled in a church with a properly functioning soul-winning program.

To Win the Lost to Christ

We are not merely talking about making contacts or developing relationships, but by God's grace and in the power of His Spirit, you and your church will see people throughout your town personally accepting Christ.

To Saturate Our Community With the Gospel

In the past four years our church family in Lancaster, California have personally contacted every home in our community at least two times. We have either spoken to the residents or left the Gospel in printed form at every home.

I believe in the philosophy of saturation. I believe God's people are encouraged by seeing the map of our city shaded in as the church family systematically visits each home. I realize the "church growth experts" belittle this approach as antiquated, yet Acts 20:20 speaks of ministry being both public and "from house to house." Even before the cults began taking their false doctrine to the streets, God's people were sharing Christ with much boldness.

To Train and Equip God's People

Of course the soul-winning program is more than an outreach ministry; it is also a teaching ministry. My experience has been that soul-winning Christians typically grow in their Bible knowledge at an accelerated rate because they are often asked to give answers for the reason of their faith. Of course, the key person in leading the training effort must be the pastor. The pastor must train not only by way of his verbal teaching but also by his active example in ministry. Often the larger a church grows and the greater the administrative responsibilities become, the greater is the challenge for the pastor to lead the way in personally going out into the community. Yet this is the responsibility of leadership. We must lead the way by example.

The Function of the Soul-Winning Ministry

I recommend that each pastor or church leader establish a special night to "kick off" the soul-winning program. The second Tuesday night of September has been a good time for my church, as it is a time when families are getting back on schedule after summertime. Prior to this special night there should be ample promotion from the pastor, as well as personal enlist-ment. I recommend that a dinner be served before the program is presented, and it is a good idea to encourage the church family to sign up for the dinner. We have tried to budget in such a way that there is no charge for the dinner.

We must
lead the way
by example.

After the meal, all church workers, previously trained soul winners and newly enlisted soul winners may proceed to an adjacent meeting room.

Personally, I prefer to use the church auditorium because the use of this room implies the meeting is an important meeting. Frankly, this kickoff meeting is the highlight of the calendar year for me as a pastor, because I believe Christ is pleased to see people gathered, not merely desiring to have their "felt needs" met, but desiring to go out with the Word of Christ and meet the single most important need of others.

TEAM Soul Winning

At this time we introduce the soul-winning program of our church. We call the program TEAM Soul Winning. TEAM stands for: Train • Every • Available • Member.

Of course this is the objective of the program, and I believe every pastor will be thrilled as he sees a membership equipped for this great task.

The TEAM Soul-Winning program is comprised of two basic groups of people. The first group is called TEAM 1, and their primary involvement is in first-time contacts and house-to-house calling. The TEAM 2 group focuses on follow-up calls to those who have previously visited the church or been contacted in another way.

The kickoff meeting usually includes a message to challenge hearts for souls. This message should be brief and relevant to the night. Also at the kickoff meeting we explain that these TEAMs meet on Tuesdays and Saturdays, and we also explain the basic operation of what to expect at the weekly soul-winning meetings. This explanation is given, along with handouts and notepaper.

The Organized Soul-Winning Meeting

Every soul-winning meeting should be well prepared prior to the arrival of the church members. Probably one of the most important aspects of our organization process is the supply table. This table not only provides needed forms, it also makes a statement about your seriousness in this matter of reaching people! The following items should be present at the table.

The Soul-Winning Supply Table

1. Sign-in Sheets—Every TEAM member is registered at the kickoff night and encouraged to sign in at his weekly meeting. This allows the leader of the soul-winning program to encourage the faithful and nurture the weary along the way. It is also on this sheet where the soul winner records the total number of contacts made when he returns.

2. Maps—I do not believe the best approach in reaching a city for Christ is the "go wherever" approach. We give each team a map with a specific street highlighted. If someone on that street has requested we not visit his home, we indicate the address on the map page with instructions not to visit that home. Also on the map page there is provided a place for comments.

This is where a soul winner informs the leader of the ministry of any potential good follow-up call for later in the week or any difficult situation worthy of record. The maps are to be placed in the "complete" or "incomplete" box at the end of the evening or morning of calling.

3. Decision Cards—Of course every decision is to be recorded and turned back in to the soul-winning director. Most soul winners are encouraged to make their own follow-up calls; however, it may be more relevant for someone else to make the follow-up call. For example, it may be that the person who made the decision is a young adult who can be referred to the young adults' teacher. Other instances may involve a lady who might feel more comfortable receiving a follow-up visit from a lady her age or a teacher of a ladies' Sunday school class.

> Your planning makes a statement about your seriousness to reach people!

4. Gospel Tracts—Quality brochures explaining the truth of the Gospel and presenting a clear gospel message. Since what we believe is the most important truth anyone will ever read, then our printed materials should reflect that fact. Over the years we have worked hard at developing printed materials that God will bless. These materials are available for use by other churches, and many have used them successfully in reaching their communities with the Gospel. (For a sample catalog contact, *Truth for Today Publications* • 4020 East Lancaster Blvd. • Lancaster, CA 93535 • 800-68-TODAY.)

5. Specialty Tracts—We provide brochures written especially for Catholics. We also provide brochures which are printed in Spanish, as well as brochures teaching the importance of baptism.

6. Team 2 Follow-Up Calls—Although the leader will normally distribute ahead of time the best follow-up calls to appropriate teachers or seasoned soul winners, there should be a tray filled with follow-up calls from various contacts (i.e., new move-ins, parents of children who visited, contacts from TEAM 1 house-to-house visitation).

7. City Maps

8. Gifts—We also recommend each church provide gifts, such as a coffee mug or flashlight for the "new move-in visits." Periodically we have used a brief video presentation about our church as a gift for newcomers.

The Soul-Winning Lesson

In addition to the soul-winning table, the ministry leader should prepare a lesson for the purpose of training the soul winners. The training in our ministry is comprised of Track I and Track II meetings. For example, our Tuesday night program meets at 6:30 p.m. If a person has just enrolled in the program at the kickoff meeting the week prior, he would attend the Track I training lessons. The Track I lessons are found in this book and typically require 25 to 35 weeks of instruction, depending upon the calendar of the individual local church.

The Track II training is for graduates of Track I, and these lessons deal with how to witness to people from various religions and cult backgrounds. An occasional refresher of the basics of soul winning is taught to this group as well. During the summer months, we combine the two groups and teach important lessons from the Gospels and the book of Acts, which have a soul-winning theme.

Creating Soul-Winning Partners

It is vital that the pastor or ministry leader take a personal interest in helping to pair the new soul winners with those who can mentor and train them as they go out into the harvest field. The process of pairing takes place in two ways:

First—Many mature believers are friends with less mature Christians whom they will be responsible to train.

Second—The pastor or TEAM leader will review the new registrants after the kickoff meeting and help by assigning the new soul winners to partners. Normally this is done just prior to the first training meeting.

The principle of having a partner in ministry is well established in Scripture. It was the Holy Spirit who instructed the church at Antioch to separate Paul and Barnabas for the first missionary journey. The encouragement and accountability which these partnerships provide are truly a blessing.

Overseeing the Soul-Winning Program

Of course, any ministry of a local church will rise or fall depending upon the spiritual leadership which the ministry is given. While the pastor must set an example in the area of soul winning, it is a blessing when another dedicated individual gives oversight to the operation of the soul-winning program.

This individual oversees and coordinates the recordkeeping of all areas of the city which have been contacted. This leader also rearranges TEAM 1 contacts to TEAM 2 soul winners, church Sunday school teachers or pastors.

This individual gives general encouragement and support to those who have become involved in the soul-winning program.

Friend, this chapter has been filled with "nuts and bolts" for organizing a soul-winning program. In conclusion, we must be reminded that it is one thing to have a plan, but it is another thing entirely to have a heart for souls. Why not stop and pray now that God would give you a heart for lost souls and a mind to develop a program which will effectively reach and win people for the Lord?

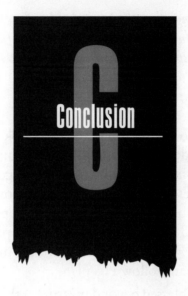

Conclusion

C

"Commit Thou

to faithful men "

"And the things that thou hast heard of me among many witnesses, the same commit thou to faithful men, who shall be able to teach others also."—II Tim. 2:2.

As we come to the final page of this book, we return to the original theme of developing a soul-winning ministry. We must be continually teaching faithful men who can go and teach other faithful men. These pages have taken shape over almost twenty years of ministry, and they have been proven to be both Biblical and effective. God is so faithful to fulfill His promises, bless His people, and build His church when hearts are turned toward Him and when Christians follow His plan.

We have been blessed beyond measure at the Lancaster Baptist Church. God's hand has been so evident, and His blessings, so marvelous. At times we as a church family have simply had to wonder in amazement and finally utter, "This is the LORD's doing; it is marvellous in our eyes" (Ps. 118:23).

The pages of this book represent our best effort to put words to what we have seen God bless for the last twelve years of ministry. Seeing souls saved, new Christians grounded, and a church family established for God's glory is a wonderful and fantastic thrill. It is a wonderful journey. Seeing those Christians move on to maturity in leading and discipling others is beyond wonderful—it is in reality God's touch.

From our heart to yours, we wish you God's greatest blessings as you apply the truths of God's Word to your personal life and to your church family. May God richly reward you as you become a winner and builder of committed followers of Jesus Christ!

Sincerely,
Pastor Paul Chappell
February 1998

For a complete list of books available from the Sword of the Lord, write to Sword of the Lord Publishers, P. O. Box 1099, Murfreesboro, Tennessee 37133.

(800) 251-4100
(615) 893-6700
FAX (615) 848-6943
E-mail: 102657.3622@compuserve.com

Truth for Today Publications

Truth for Today Publications is a publications ministry offering high-quality brochures, tracts and flyers, as well as a full graphic design service, to meet the needs of independent Baptist churches. For more information and a free sample packet of available resources, or for information about other books by Dr. Chappell, please call toll-free (800) 688-6329.

WEST COAST BAPTIST COLLEGE

West Coast Baptist College is a fundamental Baptist Bible college that is a ministry of Lancaster Baptist Church in Lancaster, California. West Coast Baptist College offers full four-year degrees in ministry majors and is dedicated to equipping and training young leaders for the 21st century. For a complimentary video and info packet, please call (888) 694-9222.